658.409

KV-749-922

Managing in the Single European Market

Managing in the Single European Market

Richard Brown

*Published in association with
the Institute of Management*

Butterworth-Heinemann Ltd
Linacre House, Jordan Hill, Oxford OX2 8DP

℞ A member of the Reed Elsevier plc group

OXFORD LONDON BOSTON
MUNICH NEW DELHI SINGAPORE SYDNEY
TOKYO TORONTO WELLINGTON

First published 1993
Reprinted 1994

British Library Cataloguing in Publication Data
Brown, Richard
   Managing in the Single Market
   I. Title
   658

ISBN 0 7506 1575 3

Printed and bound in Great Britain by Clays Ltd, St Ives plc

Contents

Figures and tables

Figures

Tables

About the author

Richard Brown is Deputy Director General for the British Chambers of Commerce (BCC) with wide-ranging representational responsibilities towards government institutions in the UK and European Community. The British Chambers of Commerce are the largest business representative body in the United Kingdom. Prior to this he was head of external policy at the British Institute of Management, specializing in business legislation, particularly in the EC. A frequent public commentator, he has addressed audiences across Europe, as well as on radio and television, and select committees, on such issues as economic policy, industrial relations and trade with the EC. A graduate in modern languages from the University of East Anglia, he has lived and worked in France at the OECD, and in Switzerland as a teacher.

He is the editor of the weekly journal *Business Briefing*, and is a member of the advisory committee of the Central Statistical Office.

His publications include six BIM reports, and more than two hundred articles. This is his fourth book dealing with the European Community.

Preface

The book enables managers and students of management to gain the relevant knowledge, context and insight into the theory, principles and effects of the European single market, against which to apply their management competences. Managing in the single market does not require many new skills or faculties; the principles of sound management remain in place under whatever circumstances. Nevertheless, the completion of a single wide European market, and the further development of the European Community does require a shift in perspective, as well as a different understanding of the framework in which businesses and the public sector must operate. One element of this which is inescapable is a concentration on the management of change, but the other is more simply a different rule book and a different playing field. This book sets out the new rules, and describes the playing field. Inevitably this means that different strategies, tactics and operations will be appropriate, both at home and abroad. These are suggested, but there is no blueprint for effective management of an organization in the European context. We can be sure that the way managers have managed to date is unlikely to be suitable for the changed environment, but it remains above all part of the management function for individual managers to assess their own responses.

Exploring the different aspects of the European Community's activities, this book aims to provide an understanding of how the functions of managers are affected by the establishment of the wider market place, and by such apparently esoteric phenomena as economic clustering, pan-Europeanism and spatial coherence. Clearly demonstrating in a straightforward way how such opaque policies as 'economic cohesion' have a very real impact on all managers, the book explores the past and future development of the EC from the perspective of practising managers. These are not simply political slogans, but policies which require action. This is not a guide book to doing business in Europe, nor does it seek to be an introduction to management. There are sufficient works of these kinds available (some of which are noted in the Bibliography). I have sought to set out in practical terms the ways in which the responses of buyers and sellers, producers and distributors, financiers and manufacturers, researchers, and professionals should be geared to the new environment.

Already equipped with, or learning, the core management competences, this book takes the reader through the steps to understanding how those competences can be applied in the new and changing business environment of the single European market. An understanding of the philosophies and goals, as well as an appreciation of the mechanics of the European Community will enable skilled and competent managers to apply themselves to the challenges ahead.

Above all the European Community is a fast-moving and turbulent political environment, with which it is no simple feat to keep up to date. An appreciation of the tenets of the single market provides a valuable indicator of future developments. The stresses that emerged in the European Exchange Rate Mechanism, and the uncertainty over the future of the Maastricht Treaty in the autumn of 1992 underlined the lack of stability facing managers in the European context. However, it has certainly been the case ever since the inception of the Common Market that the business community has been one or even several steps ahead of the politicians. Despite national political uncertainties and equivocation over European policies in all member states, there is an inevitability about economic convergence and a greater integration of the Community's economies.

The extent and timescale to which the Maastricht Treaty is finally implemented in all member states impinges little on the progress of the Community. The themes and goals in that treaty are all contained, perhaps to a less explicit degree, in the founding Treaty of Rome, and will continue to be pursued because they are in the interests of businesses and managers throughout the territories of the twelve, and the other European states queuing at the door to come in. Completion of the single market may only prove to be just one step towards an ever closer European union, but it remains the most important one, and a step that is now irrevocable. There is no going back. Lest any reader doubt this, look to the preparations, already well underway, for Maastricht II, another inter-governmental conference aimed at revising the treaty, in 1996.

A final point concerns the European Exchange Rate Mechanism. At the time of writing Italy and the United Kingdom have suspended their membership of the ERM following the break on Wednesday, 16 September 1992. In this observer's personal view, UK rejoining a mechanism is an inevitability only clouded by the timing and reform of the mechanism. Nevertheless, for businesses operating in this changed environment the underlying economic principles upon which the ERM is based remain, and so long as competitors remain in the system they (and the UK) cannot afford to sit back in splendid isolation while convergence is happening all around them.

Richard Brown
London, October 1992

Acknowledgement

I would like to thank Alexandra for all her support and encouragement while I wrote this book. My girlfriend when I began, and wife by the end.

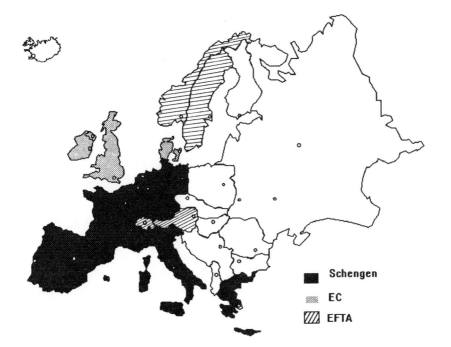

	Schengen
	EC
	EFTA

1 International trade

Trade and international trade are becoming fuzzy concepts. For most of us in the developed world everything we wear, eat, or use has been the subject of some form of trade of an increasingly international nature. Ever since the early Phoenicians set sail around the Mediterranean and discovered that somewhere there was somebody who valued their goods or services more than they did, international trade has grown. No country in the world can satisfy its consumers solely with domestically produced goods or services – or at least if it could, it is unlikely that it could do so as efficiently. The United States is probably the most self-sufficient internal economy in the world, with around 15 per cent of its GDP reliant upon international trade. Whilst this makes it susceptible to the lures, the fool's gold, of protectionism, the US remains committed to free trade, fully aware, not just of its global political responsibilities, but also the dangers of importing inflation and inefficiency.

Although the aim of the single European market (SEM) is to increase overall levels of trade between the nation member states who make up the European Communities (EC), the means by which this has happened is by obscuring its international nature. Within the EC international trade is no longer concerned with imports and exports, but 'intra-Community demand-led consumption, and intra-Community producer-led supply'. To a businessman the semantics are possibly irrelevant as the principles of international trade remain the same. This is not only true for international traders, but all business people who operate in international markets, which include home markets so long as there are foreign competitors operating there. For the United Kingdom, as an island with only limited natural resources, this is especially the case. In the twentieth century those countries which have experimented, or have been forced into isolation (in varying degrees and for varying lengths of time), such as the Inuit, Albanians, Vietnamese, and Cubans have quickly found the standards of living of their citizens falling behind, as their economies degenerate towards a system no better than that enjoyed in Europe during the Middle Ages.

The advantages of international trade are clear. Beyond our elemental needs of shelter and nourishment, there will always be things that we want, and human nature has proved remarkably reliable in always wanting more. The capacity to supply this demand is only matched by the capacity to consume it. This is the essential precursor of economic growth. In developed countries there is an almost universal acceptance that each generation will enjoy a higher standard of living than the previous one. This is a direct consequence of sustainable economic growth, and provides some explanation of why recession comes as such a shock, undermining this basic expectation. However, with limited resources − raw materials, energy, and human resource − supply needs to be efficient, and cost effective in the widest sense including time, effort, and husbandry. Thus from once supporting our needs as hunter-gatherers, man realized there had to be a better way, and developed agriculture. From thence it was only a short step to the development of barter and then trade as the work was divided and outputs shared. As the ability to travel increased so arose the benefits of international trade, which reflected the relative wealth or availability of resource, and satisfied the increasingly sophisticated and diverse wants of consumers.

Isolationists, reliant on direct production and consumption may have developed very efficient means of production, but are typified by a lack of choice for goods and services (restricted by sparse resources), and of competition between goods and services, and therefore quality. The open market trader who trades with another area unlike his own in terms of raw materials or climate will not only have access to a wider diversity of goods, but will also benefit from the principle of comparative costs,[1] and the dissemination of knowledge. The idea is that economic agents are most efficiently employed in activities in which they perform relatively better than in others. The importance of comparative advantage is that it suggests that, even if someone is very bad at some activity, perhaps even worse than any one else at it, it could still be efficient for him to pursue it if he is even more inept at other activities. The idea is particularly important in international trade, where it is suggested that countries should specialize in areas in which they have comparative advantage. Whilst political and social considerations quickly come into play, the benefits of international trade to those who take part are quickly self evident, and examples are obvious. Everybody wants bananas and cars. Caribbean islands easily and efficiently produce more bananas than are needed, but have few resources for the production of manufactured goods, such as coal or iron ore. British consumers therefore benefit from the import of bananas. To pay for these bananas we need to sell something of equal or greater value. As such this is simply a process of dividing the necessary work (labour, energy and materials) where it can most efficiently be done. It quickly leads to specialization which has its own dangers and advantages, but always enhances efficiency through economies of scale, increased skill, and use of custom equipment and tools. In turn these feed output and generate surpluses with which to pay for imports and the cycle repeats itself on the other side of the world, not only as the quest for cheaper resources widens, but the need for expanding market places grows beyond the bounds of a bilateral system. By the eighteenth century, more than two-thirds of cotton-based textiles produced in Britain – made entirely from imported cotton was being exported. This added value arrived at through the implementation of the latest technology, provided enormous comparative advantage, and significant wealth.

This system of comparative advantage should not be taken at face value as an example of an efficient marketplace. Bilateral trade quickly moves to a multilateral phase, demand sophistication increases, and imbalances swiftly arise. The balance of payments between different countries (or regions) is of some significance, even within a trading bloc where there are no barriers, and the payment still needs to be made to account for the flow of goods or services in either direction. In a modern economy payment can be made through technical measures such as high interest rates, or standing debt, which reflect to a certain extent the premium or penalty on that country through the value of its currency, or artificial changes in the value of that currency. These penalties inevitably give rise to political and social problems, as well as economic hardship, and frequently manifest themselves through rising inflation and or unemployment.

In response to this, artificial structures aimed at redressing the imbalances have been imposed in the blunt form of tariffs, which remove the comparative advantage by making a good or service equal to or more expensive than that produced at home, or non-tariff barriers, such as differing technical standards, or red-tape

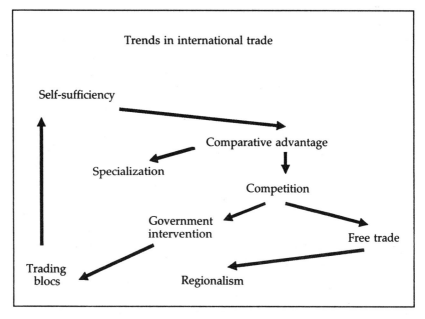

Figure 1.1 *Trends in international competitiveness*

which are designed to make it difficult, or at least more costly to import goods. In this way, the home producer remains protected from competition, but the consumer gets no benefit from the ability of the foreign producer's ability to deliver a good more cheaply, and suffers from a lack of choice. Enjoying a quasi-monopoly the home producer has little incentive to become more efficient, or to diversify.

The social implications of free and competitive marketplaces have always led politicians to interfere to at least some extent. There will never be a truly free market. Apart from social considerations, there remain national implications for defence, for so-called essential services, for industries of 'strategic importance', such as farming and coal-mining. A free market will only ever be possible in a democracy, and it will always prove too great a temptation for politicians in a democracy to resist intervening (especially when economic cycles are not in synchrony with political cycles) to address the immediate consequences of trade imbalances as they affect their electorate. Indeed it is a fundamental tenet of a social market economy (the underlying basis of the European Community) that the framework provided by government in which the market can operate can only be sustained by regular elections. This in itself leads to market imperfections, which governments seek to correct. The important point to understand therefore is that markets will always be political by nature. Against this background we can understand the development of the European Community, its operations, and how best to plan within such a framework.

Even at this stage in the development of the western plural society, with the demise of the centrally planned economy, there is yet to be a clear consensus on the role of government (if any) in managing international trade. There is a widespread understanding, or at least appreciation, epitomized in the General Agreement on Tariffs and Trade (GATT),[2] that freer markets are in everyone's interest, but putting that into practice is somewhat harder.

The economic levers in the hands of politicians are numerous, including nationalization, price and wage controls, subsidy, discriminatory public purchasing policies, economic sanctions, and legal barriers to the movement of goods, services or money. In order to provide a more stable and competitive business environment it is an imperative of the European Community to remove the potential of national politicians from exercising these levers to gain comparative — but unfair — advantage for a particular country, region or sector.

If we look at the outcomes of comparative advantage in less abstract terms we can see the immediate impacts on individual businesses, and therefore rationalize to some extent the development of the single European market. Essentially, the factors at play so far identified are: increased potential market size; a geographical diversity; greater opportunities for specialization and varying external influences. The opportunities and benefits for the trading organization in extending its operations to an international level become clear: economies of scale can be arrived at from the larger market; new products can be derived from a greater diversity of resources, and to meet a greater diversity of demand; scope for specialization increases with the size of a market − a market of 60 million people may not be enough to warrant manufacturing a left handed instrument, for example, but one of 340 million may well prove worth the investment; and the opportunity to derive expertise and different comparative advantage (such as a more efficient transport and distribution infrastructure) from a wider geography. The establishment of the single market introduces other opportunities for growth, but these will be raised in later chapters. The process of internationalization is clearly underway.

A recent survey of 400 middle market companies in 20 developed countries revealed that 86 per cent of all companies interviewed are selling outside their home country, and 49 per cent have established manufacturing operations at home.[3] The reasons given include growth opportunities, less dependence on the home economy, and customer demand. Deterrents to internationalization identified by the Deloitte report included likely profitability being too low, and the lack of a suitable business partner.

If the benefits of international trade are now well understood and accepted by economists, businessmen and politicians, then the benefits derived from *free* international trade are even greater, and lie at the heart of both the GATT negotiations and the European single market. The Organization for Economic Cooperation and Development (OECD) estimates that obstacles to free international trade are seriously distorting trading patterns, the allocation of resources, and international growth. The total economic costs of these barriers are estimated to exceed $475 billion per annum.[4] A successful conclusion of the Uruguay Round would add around $195 billion per annum to world income, or about 50 per cent of the income of China. For the European Community, the OECD model predicts a 2.4 per cent growth in GDP in 2002 resulting from a successful GATT negotiation.

OECD points out the causes of imbalances driving the desire for protectionism:

> In many countries, excess capacity in traditional industries, and intense competitive pressures in these and more modern sectors, such as electronics, from emerging industrial competitors, has provided an impetus for strengthening protectionism. Politically, governments in the industrialized countries appear insecure, with the governing parties or coalitions vulnerable to small swings in support.[5]

It is inevitable that an economic, or commercial consideration of the single market quickly becomes entangled with political considerations, but the above provides the rationale for the development of, and need to stimulate, international trade, and points to some of the problems – principally market failures – which the establishment of the single market seeks to address. Because of this entanglement the development of the EC will be bound up with important questions about centralism, federalism and subsidiarity. These are important issues which impact on the business community and will be addressed later. In the meantime, there is agreement (at least at a political if not practical level) on the basic tenets of the Community. An unshakeable faith in capitalism provides the starting point, coupled with the belief that the main engine of economic growth is competition. From this springs the need for innovation, and quality. Competition is the mechanism by which the market rewards those who supply demand, and penalizes the inefficient.

Table 1.1 Definition of subsidiarity

Article 3b of the Treaty on European Union prescribes that the Community shall act within the limits of the powers conferred upon it. In areas which do not fall within its exclusive competence, the Community shall take action, in accordance with the principle of subsidiarity, only if and in so far as the objectives of the proposed action cannot be sufficiently achieved by the Member States and can therefore, by reason of the scale or effects of the proposed action, be better achieved by the Community.

Free markets and competition are not, however, an unfailing lodestar. It is, of course, debatable (and probably irresolvable) whether market failure is caused by government intervention, or whether government intervention is necessary because of market failure but in any case there are clear failures of the market to meet the wider needs of consumers and citizens. Commerce and industry have tended to adopt a shorter term outlook than prudence and efficiency would suggest. This is in large part due to the structures of ownership in the economy. Factors like protecting the environment are intractable when left entirely to a market which cannot discount the value, or calculate the premium on environmental protection, unless it is externalized, and made transparent by such mechanisms as taxation. Large scale infrastructure or education projects do not provide a quick enough direct return on investment to be attractive to the profit motive of individuals. Social values such as care of the elderly, and high standards of health and safety are unlikely to be met by purely economic and commercial forces, requiring political redress. These then are legitimate areas for government, and therefore provide the second issue which businesses must address in the new framework of the single European market: the need to conform with a different structure of law and regulation, as well as new market forces. Controversially the opportunity is being taken to impose some measure of social responsibility on businesses. This paradox remains unresolved and will continue to lead to potential fundamental disagreements at Community level. This blend of the quest for economic growth, and a higher quality of life is a difficult balance to keep, but is the essence of the European Communities. Article 2 of the founding Treaty of Rome states:

> It shall be the aim of the Community, by establishing a Common Market and progressively approximating the economic policies of Member States, to promote throughout the Community, a harmonious development of economic activities, a continuous and balanced expansion, an increased stability, an accelerated raising of the standard of living and closer relations between Member States.[6]

This provides an even wider definition of the European Community beyond that of a single internal market. Indeed, the President of the European Commission, rather too honestly than political considerations may have required, made clear that it would not be long before 80 per cent of all economic and social legislation would be derived from Brussels.

With competition policy as the motor, the framework of the Community extends to all areas which impact on commercial activity: regional policy, employment law, consumer protection, transport, communications, and the environment. How these policy areas impact on businesses themselves will be explored in later chapters.

It may, however, be useful at this stage to consider briefly just the single aspect of regionalism. Completion of a single market is a means to maximizing the advantages of free international trade, by dismissing the very notion of international trade between different countries. The result is not, however, simply to substitute inter-regional for international trade, but to manipulate, or at least alter the conditions by which flows of employment, skills, means of production and capital move within the trading bloc in order to ensure that there is greater competition between regions for capital and human resources. This brings to light an inherent contradiction in the single market philosophy. The advantages of free trade are most apparent when there are marked differences between trading areas, and yet the European Community is set on a policy of regional convergence aimed at eradicating these differences, particularly in the context of structures such as economic and monetary union. Barriers to trade have, to date, ensured that regional divergence has remained large. The top ten regions in the EC have a local GDP of two and half times as great as the bottom ten.[7] This is not simply of academic interest, but a factor which is likely to affect the business planning of all firms in the European Community. There is ample evidence that the migrations of production from one region to another are stimulated by divergent conditions. Few UK companies, for example, have been moved to set up manufacturing plants overseas to benefit from lower wage costs, unit labour costs in the UK being amongst the lowest in the EC. The relocation of Hoover's production plants from France to the United Kingdom is a case in point, clearly demonstrating the enhanced mobility of the means of production to more favourable locations. Indeed, the British Government has made considerable efforts to draw the attention of potential inward investors to the low-cost nature of labour in the UK. Removal of the barriers to trade is likely to change the basis for competitive advantage, and so encourage an even greater concentration of wealth in some regions to the detriment of others, particularly those on the geographic periphery of the European Community.[8]

The most direct impact on commerce and industry is likely to lie in locational decisions concerned with being close to customers, raw materials, or appropriately skilled labour. With the lack of an even dispersion of economic activity, industry will inevitably be drawn to economic 'hotspots'. Identifying these will form a major plank of any company's strategy for the single market.

Economic clustering is not a new phenomenon. Indeed it has been most evident at times of major industrial change. The industrial revolution brought with it self-evident centres of activity in particular sectors, which have been reinforced by a clustering of secondary industries. Steel manufacture in Sheffield, paper in Sweden, clocks in Switzerland, ceramics in Italy are all examples stemming from the industrial revolution. More recently there have been newer clusters such as the information technology centres in Silicon Valley where companies are drawn by concentrations of skilled labour, an appropriate service sector in place, the possibility of suitable partners for collaboration and other factors.

New clusters or hotspots can be expected to develop across the EC in spite of policies aimed at regional convergence. Pools of skilled labour will attract capital and companies, widening and developing new skills over time; customer awareness will draw in markets, driving innovation and competitiveness. The economic arguments for and against clustering are unresolved. Any casual western visitor to the Middle East is immediately struck by the same phenomenon on a local scale: whole streets of bakers all competing with each other, for example. Whilst the macro-economic consequences of clustering, such as social dumping, are significant, business will have to make decisions in the light of these clusters. Should they join in, locate at an economic hotspot and take advantage of the pools of labour and concentration of support service industries, or avoid them, and benefit from cheaper labour for example? Lagging regions, outside of the clusters are often typified by high unemployment, low qualifications, and poor networks for communications and energy, but they also tend to benefit from a high degree of government intervention (at both a national and European level), and often from policies of deregulation (enterprise zones etc.).

A final factor worth considering at this stage is the emergence of trading blocs. These structures have been in existence for decades. Some such as Comecon have broken up, some such as EFTA[9] are dwindling in importance, others have purely political motives such as the Cairns Group, and OPEC, others have sound economic reasons such as the EC and ASEAN,[10] and possibly NAFTA.[11] Many other nascent trading blocs in the Arab and African nations are emerging. Nevertheless the trend is a clear one. It is possible that the world will once again divide into three or four trading blocs, each with considerable powers.

There are considerable dangers that the emergence of powerful trading blocs will do little to stimulate international trade, as they increasingly resort to protectionism by discriminating against others – an option made possible by the self-sufficiency which arises from the size of the bloc. In part the development of rival trading blocs has been a response to the EC internal market programme, which many perceived as simply one which whilst removing barriers to trade within the Community, was an excuse to erect even greater barriers around the Community. The so-called 'Fortress Europe' has been denied, and indeed considerable efforts have gone into forging bilateral and multilateral trade agreements between the EC and developing countries.[12] Much inward investment into the Community – particularly Japanese investment in the United Kingdom – has been stimulated by this fear of fortress Europe. Non-EC companies seeking to develop markets inside the Community see the establishment of 'screw-driver' assembly plants within the EC as a way around any potential barriers. This blurring of internationalism – is a Japanese car factory in Sunderland, employing UK workers, but using pre-manufactured imports, really producing EC cars? – is increasingly contentious with some member states, such as France calling for quotas, and others taking a more reasonable, but still dangerously interventionist view about defining minimum local content rules in terms of added value.

Table 1.2 *Intra-Community imports and exports % of trade which is EC oriented*

	Import	Export	Balance
Belgium/Luxembourg	74	72	−2
Denmark	52	49	−3
France	61	60	−1
Greece	62	67	+5
Ireland	66	74	+8
Italy	57	56	−1
Netherlands	64	75	+11
Portugal	63	68	+5
Spain	55	64	−9
UK	53	59	−6
Germany	53	53	0

Source: Euromonitor

Michael Heseltine describes the European Community as 'a triumph for capitalism'[13] and this can no longer be seriously doubted in the light of the considerable economic lag suffered by centrally planned economies. Nevertheless the development of the EC will be characterized by an on-going tension between those pushing the free-market principles of increasing competition and deregulation, and the politically motivated interventionists who seek to push forward direct policies for industry, social programmes, and constraints on business. For the business manager planning a strategy for operations in the European arena, these tensions should be noticed, and indeed taken advantage of while the Community continues to evolve.

To conclude this introduction a perspective on the position of the UK as an international trader clearly shows the extent to which there are opportunities for British businesses in the European Community. More than £100 billion worth of goods are traded between the UK and other EC member states, i.e. just over half of our imports and exports, and around a quarter of our GDP. Whilst this may be demonstrative of a balance between self-sufficiency and exploitation of the opportunities of international trade, it is also a measure of our own comparative advantage, and when compared with other member states underlines our ability to maximize and improve that advantage.

2 The development of the European Community

As has already been established, even though we speak of the European *Economic* Community, the European Community (EC)[14] is an essentially political structure, which was developed as a response to the continuing political dislocation in Europe during the first half of the twentieth century. Whatever the causes of the First World War it is, in retrospect, clear that it simply laid the foundations for competing extremes of political thought. If the Second World War was the response to the rise of fascism in Europe, then the vision of a united Europe – first put forward by Winston Churchill, was a response to that war. By tying the economic prosperity of the European nations to each other, it was envisaged that there would be fewer opportunities for aggression, and an end to the sorts of fragmentation suffered after the First World War. That this has proved to be the case is now irrefutable, but needs to be acknowledged if we are to understand the preoccupation of those leading the development of the Community with issues of a non-economic nature. The quest for political union, and common security policies, all impact on the economic life of Europe's businessmen, but are not motivated solely by the desire to create a free market.

The Treaty of Rome which came into force on 1 January 1958 was signed by France, West Germany, Italy, Belgium, The Netherlands and Luxembourg and is the cornerstone of the development of the EC. Essentially it established a common customs union, and set out a timetable – long since ignored – for the abolition of obstacles to movement of capital, goods, services and labour between the six signatories. At the time this was a visionary move which went beyond the establishment of simply a free trading area, as the problems of distorted competition through such mechanisms as dumping, monopolies and subsidy were foreseen and addressed in the treaty. The treaty established the institutional structures of the Communities, and has paved the way for a greater sophistication in its political framework. New bodies such as the European Investment Bank, merger with the European Coal and Steel Community, and Euratom, development of structures such as the common agricultural policy, the Lomé Convention, the European Monetary System, the European Economic Area, amendments such as the Single European Act and the Treaty on European Union, as well as enlargement have vastly extended the ambit of the EC, in a manner which is both wider, and thus encompassing more areas of economic and social activity, and deeper by having greater and more detailed influence throughout the territories of the Community. The task of the European Community is a wide one:

> The Community shall have as its task, by establishing a common market and monetary union and by implementing common policies or activities, to promote throughout the Community a harmonious and balanced development of economic activities, sustainable and non-inflationary growth respecting the environment, a high degree of convergence of economic performance, a high level of employment and of social protection, the raising of the standard of living and quality of life, and economic and social cohesion and solidarity among Member States.[15]

This has been essentially a political development, which many now consider to be unstoppable. Nevertheless, the hybrid nature of the development of the Communities has left it with a complex framework of law, unclear relationships with national legislatures, and an unwieldy decision-making structure. Conflicting demands, such as the needs to address the 'democratic deficit'[16] and the desire to improve the decision-making processes, or the need to respect the principle of subsidiarity at the same time as removing obstacles to trade have resulted in political tensions which have hampered the development of the single European market. This very hybrid nature also gives rise to expectations of a 'two-speed Europe', with some member states proceeding quickly with some aspects, but slower in others. It is now almost the case that businesses are continually being reminded that although the purpose of the single market is to develop international trade and thus economic growth, it has not been done for the benefit of businesses alone, and there is a price to be paid to the wider community.

The institutions of the Community have been designed to provide a political system of checks and balances, where different bodies have discrete powers. The abilities of each body are held in check by the others. This has proved to be more evolutive than envisaged by the EC's founders, and is likely to continue to change to meet the developmental processes of widening, and deepening, and ebbs and flows, of political consensus. The principal institutions as defined by Article 4 of the treaty are:

- The Council of Ministers
- The Commission
- The European Parliament (EP)
- The European Court of Justice (ECJ)
- The European Court of Auditors

There are also consultative bodies:

Table 2.1 Activities of the European Community

1 The elimination, as between member states, of customs duties and quantative restrictions on the import and export of goods, and all other measures having equivalent effect;
2 a common commercial policy;
3 an internal market characterized by the abolition, as between member states, of obstacles to the free movement of goods, persons, services and capital;
4 measures concerning the entry and movement in the internal market;
5 a common policy in the sphere of agriculture and fisheries;
6 a common policy in the sphere of transport;
7 a system ensuring that the completion of the internal market is not distorted;
8 the approximation of the laws of member states to the extent required for the functioning of the common market;
9 a policy in the social sphere comprising a European Social Fund;
10 the strengthening of economic and social cohesion;
11 a policy in the sphere of the environment;
12 the strengthening of the competitiveness of Community industry;
13 the promotion of research and technological development;
14 encouragement for the establishment and development of trans-European networks;
15 a contribution to the attainment of a high level of health protection;
16 a contribution to education and training of quality and to the flowering of cultures of the member states;
17 a policy in the sphere of development cooperation;
18 the association of the overseas countries and territories in order to increase trade and promote jointly economic and social development;
19 a contribution to the strengthening of consumer protection;
20 measures in the spheres of energy, civil protection and tourism.

- The Economic and Social Committee (ESC)
- The Committee of Regions (COR)
- The Committee of Permanent Representatives (COREPER)

Agencies:

- The European Standards Centre (CEN)
- The European Electrical and Electronics Standards Centre (CENELEC)
- The European Centre for Education and Professional Development (CEDEFOP)
- The European Investment Bank (EIB)
- The European System of Central Banks (ECSB)
- The European Monetary Institute (EMI)

Several hundred programmes including:

- ESPRIT

- EUREKA
- COMETT
- LINGUA

Structural funds:

- The European Social Fund (ESF)
- The European Regional Development Fund (ERDF)
- The European Agricultural Guidance and Guarantee Fund (EAGGF)
- The Fisheries Industry Guidance Fund (FIGF)
- The Cohesion Fund

Essentially the system is simple enough: it is the role of the European Commission to propose policy and draft legislation; the European Parliament and consultative committees have a say, the Council of Ministers makes the decision, and national governments, or the EC agencies put those decisions into effect. It is quickly evident that, at a political level, there will be conflicts, and there is therefore a referee: the European Court of Justice which acts as arbiter between those institutions. The power and influence within the Community is finely dispersed, with the Commission currently having the sole right of proposal, the Council having the sole right of decision, the Parliament being able to sack the Commission (but only limited powers of influence), and the Court being able to overturn the decisions of the Council. This would seem to make the Court the most important institution, and indeed even a cursory examination of the development of the EC shows that the major evolutionary steps forward can be traced back to landmark judgements from the European Court of Justice.

There is little that is new in the concept of a single market that was not contained in the original Treaty of Rome. What changed was a landmark decision of the ECJ involving the export of Cassis de Dijon, where the Court ruled that Germany could not put up barriers to the import of French Cassis in order to protect domestic interests. The decision established a precedent for the principle of non-discrimination in the Community, and laid the foundations for what has developed into a system of mutual recognition. Basically the judgement made clear that if a product can legally be sold in one member state, then it can be sold legally in another, without discriminating conditions attached to that sale. The whole of the single European market stems from this precept. The judgement, at a stroke, made all discriminatory tax regimes, standards, and bureaucracy prima facie contra the Treaty of Rome, and it only needed suitable legislation to be framed and agreed for them to be made illegal. The Commissioner responsible for internal trade, Lord Cockfield, listed some 300 legislative measures which were necessary to remove discriminatory regimes, anti-competitive practices, and other non-tariff barriers. (Internal tariff barriers having already been made illegal when the common customs area has established the Common External Tariff.) These he published in a White Paper which is the blueprint for the Single European Market.[17]

In practice, however, the EC displays itself, and indeed behaves very much in the manner of a large democratic but sovereign state, with its own constitution and systems of checks and balances. The 'constitution' of the EC is the Treaty of Rome, as amended by the Single European Act and the Treaty on European Union (the 'Maastricht' Treaty). In business parlance these are the Articles of Association which define the legitimate bodies and powers of the organization, as well as the manner in which decisions can be made. It is important to have at least a basic understanding of this. The EC is a living organism which will continue to develop and evolve. An understanding of the decision-making processes will allow business managers to make informed decisions about the likelihood of Community proposals becoming law. The UK business-man is at a considerable handicap in his information systems about EC developments. A media which is largely 'anti-European' has over recent years tended to confine itself to reporting, and indeed mis-reporting some of the more eccentric and particular develop-ments in the EC. A proposal, for example, to set down Europe-wide standards for food additives, so as to free the market from differing national standards, is presented in many parts of the UK media, as a proposal to ban flavoured crisps in the UK. A similar proposal defining the minimum cocoa content in chocolate confectionery, put forward for similar reasons, was similarly decried as an attack on the great British milk chocolate. There are numerous examples but each underlies the need of UK businesses to keep informed and understand the processes involved.

The treaties define the manner in which proposals can become EC law, and there are several different routes, but only two essential differences: a Commission proposal requires either unanimity in the Council of Ministers, or simply a Qualified Majority Vote (QMV) for acceptance. Where a businessman learns of a new proposal likely to affect his business, this is the immediate factor to be ascertained. This basic knowledge will give some indication of the likelihood of a proposal eventually becoming law. Some proposals which require unanimity have been on the table for more than twenty years.

At its inception, the European Community chose to move forward on the basis of consensus. No member state was to be forced to do anything it did not choose to. With only six members this proved sustainable for some time, but as the scope of the Community as well as its size enlarged it proved to be difficult to reach consen-sus on many issues. For a while, the Luxembourg Compromise, engineered by General de Gaulle, sustained the basic principle allowing one member state to opt-out of a decision where vital interests were at stake, but quickly the Community was gripped

Table 2.2   The Maastricht Treaty

What is in the Treaty on European Union
Citizenship of the Union
Community policies
Capital payments
Competition and taxation
Economic policy
Monetary policy
European Central Bank
Economic and Monetary Institute
Common commercial policy
Social policy
Education, vocational training and youth
Culture
Public health
Consumer protection
Trans-European networks
Industry
Economic and social cohesion
Research and technological development
Environment
Development cooperation
Institutions of the Community
Common foreign and security policy
Cooperation in the fields of justice
17 protocols
33 declarations

Table 2.3   Voting in the Council of Ministers

Qualified majority voting	
Belgium	5
Denmark	3
Germany	10
Greece	5
Spain	8
France	10
Ireland	3
Italy	10
Luxembourg	2
Netherlands	5
Portugal	5
United Kingdom	10
Total	76
Qualified majority	54

with a sclerotic decision-making process where progress was being increasingly vetoed. To avoid a proposal being vetoed, the Commission would, in some cases, not bring something to a vote, leaving an important piece of draft Community law wallowing in working parties and committees. There are many drafts and redrafts, such as the Fifth Company Law Directive, which are now more than twenty years old! The Single European Act and the Treaty on European Union have widened the scope of majority decision making to most areas of Community activity. Indeed it is now the rule rather than the exception. Before looking at the procedures it is worth examining, briefly, the institutions.

The European Commission is the prime mover in the Community. Although in theory not the most powerful, in practice it represents the centre of European affairs. Its main source of influence lies in its exclusive right to propose legislation. As such it is a very different institution beyond simply a civil service. It is also responsible for the administration of the Community's budget, including the structural funds, and significantly polices implementation of the treaty; applying moral pressure on member states to enact directives, and draconian fiscal penalties on companies breaching competition rules.

The Commission is made up of seventeen Commissioners; one from each member state and two from the larger ones (UK, Germany, France, Italy and Spain). Each heads up one or more directorates. The seventeen Commissioners, who are not supposed to represent national interests are supported by 11,000 staff, three-quarters of whom are administrators such as translators, interpreters and printers. Only nationals of member states may be members of the Commission, which must include at least one national of each of the member states, but not more than two. The members of the Commission are bound by the treaty to act solely in the interest of the Community as a whole.

There are 23 directorates-general (DGs). Key DGs for the business community are DG3 – Internal Market and Industrial Affairs; DG4 – Competition; DG5 – Social Affairs; and DG23 – Small and Medium Sized Enterprises. As the proposers of legislation, formulators of policy, and designers of standards, the staff of the European Commission probably have more influence on the business community today than do British MPs or even ministers.

The Council of Ministers is the decision-making body of the Community where ministers from each member state deliberate with the assistance of COREPER (Committee of Permanent Representatives) on proposals from the Commission, and decide whether or not a proposal should be adopted and translated into national legislation. The Council consists of a representative of each member state at ministerial level authorized to commit the government of the member state. It has a president, which is taken in turns for a term of six months in cycles: between 1993 and 1998, Belgium, Denmark, Germany, Greece, Spain, France, Ireland, Italy, Luxembourg, Netherlands, Portugal and the United Kingdom, and after 1998 (although accession of new members may change the cycle), Denmark, Belgium, Greece, Germany, France, Spain, Italy, Ireland, Netherlands, Luxembourg, United Kingdom and Portugal. Subsequent to the ratification of the Single European Act the Council mostly operates on a qualified majority vote.

The European Parliament, often criticized for not making up the democratic deficit which clearly exists, does not have the same power as national parliaments, and (apart from the ability to reject the Community's budget (often done), and the power to sack the Commission (never used)) deliberates on Commission proposals, putting forward opinions, and suggesting amendments which are often ignored. The Parliament meets half of the time in Luxembourg, half of the time in Strasbourg, whilst most MEPs have their offices in Brussels. MEPs are directly elected by Community citizens under a system of proportional representation.

The European Court of Justice is the final arbiter of Community Affairs. Its decisions are binding on member states and therefore all public sector organizations. Governments, public and private sector bodies, and individuals can petition the Court. All countries of the Community, with the exception of the United Kingdom, have a clearly established code of rights. It is therefore unusual for the Court to be deciding on individual cases (apart from Commission employees suing the Commission) which do not have profound precedential consequences for national legislatures. In practice this means that non-UK EC citizens have more avenues for appeal against their own governments or judiciaries than do British citizens. The lack of any Bill of Rights in the UK implementing fundamental aspects of European Community law leaves a gap in the British legal system only filled by the European Court of Justice.

The Economic and Social Committee acts in a similar way to the European Parliament. It is made up of representatives of business, employees and other interests such as consumers and deliberates on Commission proposals, offering its opinions. Its real impact is limited, but it does provide an important forum for views to be put forward, and contributes to the quality of Community legislation.

The Committee of Regions consists of representatives of regional and local bodies who are consulted by the Council or the Commission where appropriate regional interests and involved. It issues 'opinions' in a similar manner to the Economic and Social Committee.

The decision-making procedures of the Community are inherently

Table 2.4 The cooperation procedure

1   Commission makes a proposal to the EP and the Council of Ministers;
2   Parliament gives its opinion; Council adopts a common position, acting by qualified majority;
3   Council informs EP of its common position;
4   Parliament has 3 months. It can:
    (a)   approve the common position or take no decision in which case Council then adopts the proposal;
    (b)   vote to reject the common position by an absolute majority and inform the Council which can call a meeting of the Conciliation Committee comprising equal numbers from Council and Parliament; the EP may then:
    (c)   reject again by absolute majority, so the proposal is not adopted, or
    (d)   propose amendments by an absolute majority
5   If the Parliament proposes amendments at this stage, the Council has a further three months. It may:
    (a)   approve the amended text by qualified majority except for amendments opposed by the Commission which require unanimity in the Council;
    (b)   refuse to approve, in which case the Conciliation Committee is convened again. In this case:
6   The Conciliation Committee has six weeks to work on the text. If it approves a joint text, then this is adopted as long as the EP votes in favour by a majority of votes case and the Council approves by qualified majority. Failure by either institution to approve means that the proposal is not adopted.
7   If the Conciliation Committee fails to agree, the Council has a further six weeks to confirm its original position, perhaps with some EP amendments. The Parliament then has a further six weeks following confirmation to reject the text by an absolute majority of its members.

complex resulting from their evolution, and the rapid changes in the EC. Nevertheless they provide a system allowing for businesses to have an influence and impact on what affects them. The system is known as one of 'co-decision'; essentially allowing the representatives of democratically elected governments, in the form of the Council of Ministers, and the directly-elected representatives of the European Parliament to define Community law.

It is sometimes surprising that anything is ever agreed, and indeed, there still remains considerable room for manoeuvre between member states. The Maastricht Treaty contains a number of protocols and agreements effectively allowing individual member states to opt-out of certain provisions. The legality and sustainability of such opt-outs is very questionable in practice.

The main instruments of Community law are treaty requirements; directives; regulations and recommendations:

Treaty requirements are binding on all governments, bodies, organizations and citizens of the EC. The extent to which they are directly binding remains the subject of some confusion which successive ECJ judgements have failed to clarify. Various cases have tended to widen the scope, including Helen Marshall v. Southampton Area Health Authority, an equal treatment case, where the Court ruled that the treaty was directly binding on public authorities where an item was discrete and required no further explanation. In a more recent case an Italian company successfully sued the Italian Government for failure to implement the treaty,[18] again highlighting the directly binding nature of much of the treaty.

Directives are the principal instruments of Community law, which define the scope and intention of law, and are aimed at member states. Directives need to be transposed into national law to have an effect. The directive on product liability is, for example, enacted in the UK by the Consumer Protection Act.

Regulations are more detailed, and tend to be directly binding on their targets. They do not normally require transposing into national law.

Recommendations and opinions are similar to directives, but are not binding. They have some degree of moral weight, and are generally the result of a compromise when the Council or Parliament fails to agree on a directive.

As has already been noted there has been a move away from unanimity towards qualified majorities in the decision making process. At the same time there has been a similar trend away from harmonization of law, towards approximation, and thence to mutual recognition.

With an enlarged and widened Community it has proved impossible for unanimity to be achieved on a large number of proposals, particularly technical standards. For many years, the German lawnmower manufacturing industry was successfully protected from import competition by idiosyncratic standards on noise emissions. A common European standard on noise was seen as the answer to freeing intra-community trade in lawnmowers. The 'Lawnmower Noise Directive', however, was successfully blocked by the German government for many years. Apart from the obvious problems of defining the noise standard at either the minimum of acceptability around the Community, or the maximum standard of acceptability, or the average standard, the procedures for setting standards were so slow that technological advances were outstripping the standard makers. Faced with an inability to resolve completely the highest or lowest common denominator problem, the Commission sought to make it easier by moving away from 'harmonization' (making the law the same in each member state) to 'approximation' (making the law similar in each member state). This did not, however, satisfactorily resolve the problem, and so most Community Law now revolves around the principle of mutual recognition. This means that if a product, service or qualification, meets the standards required by one member state, then it should be freely traded or accepted throughout all member states.

Mutual recognition is not the perfect solution. Whilst it goes a long way to breaking down barriers to trade, it does little to encourage economies of scale between manufacturers, and heightens concerns about low safety standards in some member states. There is, therefore a degree of testing and mutual recognition of each other's standards setters, resulting in a rise in bureaucracy.

At a political level this raises the question of subsidiarity. To what extent should the Community seek to define the details of standards and regulations? The principle of subsidiarity suggests that legislation should be defined and implemented at the lowest possible level. There is however, a trade-off between common standards and the political desire for subsidiarity, which may cause difficulties for managers. Bringing legislation down to the lowest practicable level endangers the framework of common standards. If, for example, according to the principle of subsidiarity, the EC has no role in defining the content of, say, a sausage, and this role should be left to individual member states, then the sausage exporter is left in a pre-1992 situation with twelve different sets of regulations to contend with. Similar problems arise from the tendency to get around contentious proposals using the possibility of opt-outs, either on a large scale such as the UK opt-out of the Social Chapter of the Maastricht Treaty, or on a smaller scale, such as the UK opt-out for five years from the directive on part-time work.

The final problem with Community law which faces EC managers is the question of implementation and enforcement. All legislation imposes a burden on businesses in one way or another. Responsibility for implementing Community law (i.e. transposing it into national legislation) and enforcing it lies with the national governments and authorities of each member state. If businesses in one member state are faced with rigorous enforcement of, say, health and safety or environmental protection legislation, while businesses in others are able to ignore or disregard it, then there is an immediate competitive disadvantage. For example, the machinery directive requires certain guards, baffles and hoods to be placed around moving parts of certain items of machinery. Inevitably when there are machine jams, all these safeguards need to be removed before any jam or blockage can be cleared. A down-time penalty or cost is incurred. If on the other hand, someone can simply reach an arm into a machine and clear the blockage, there is a considerable saving to the business not complying with the legislation (as well as a considerable health and safety risk to the employees concerned).

Implementation and enforcement have been a significant problem

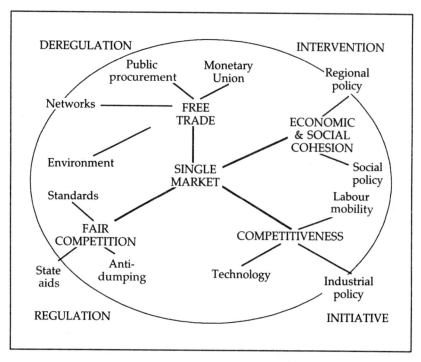

Figure 2.1 *Dynamics of the single market*

for the EC. There are few sanctions which can be brought to bear upon a member state for failures. The Maastricht Treaty includes a declaration that 'stresses that it is central to the coherence and unity of the process of European construction that each member state should fully and accurately transpose into national law the Community directives addressed to it within the deadlines laid down therein.' Nevertheless, in the face of determined campaigns to prevent the Commission from encroaching into areas of perceived sovereignty, there have been few realistic moves to improve enforcement. Enforcement remains the responsibility of the European Court of Justice, but this process takes a considerable amount of time, and again, lacks effective sanctions for failure.

Development of the Community has been an evolutive one, with the completion of the single market simply as one, albeit, important, step on the path to 'an ever closer union'.[19] The Treaty on European Union, known as the 'Maastricht Treaty' where it was signed, sets out the legal basis for the deepening, widening and enlarging of the Community and is effectively the map for managers to follow over coming years. The treaty deals with economic and political union. The implications of the former on businesses will be examined in Chapter 5. 'Political union', however, is a catch-all title which covers the development of the Community into a number of new areas which will have an impact on businesses throughout the EC.

The Maastricht Treaty covers:

Table 2.5 Development of the Community

1957	Treaty of Rome
1966	Luxembourg Compromise
1968	Common External Tariff
1973	Accession of Eire, UK and Denmark
1981	Accession of Greece
1986	Accession of Spain and Portugal
1985	Single European Act
1990	UK joins ERM
1992	Treaty on European Union signed at Maastricht
1993	Treaty ratified by all member states
1996	*Intergovernmental conference and further enlargement*

- Community decision-making
- Union citizenship
- The social dimension and development of human resources
- Economic and social cohesion
- Research and technological development
- Energy
- The environment
- Trans-European networks
- Culture and protection of heritage
- Health
- Consumer protection
- Compliance
- Vocational training and education
- Industrial policy
- Foreign and security policy

As a piece of text, it is not recommended that managers read and try to understand the treaty. It remains a legalistic document which amends the original Treaty of Rome, rather than setting out a new treaty. Nevertheless, some comprehension of the implications in certain areas is essential if managers are to be able to judge how the development of the Community will affect them and their businesses.

Citizenship of the Union is granted to any person holding nationality of a member state. This gives all individuals the rights to vote anywhere in the EC, as well as to such services as consular protection outside of the Community. The Treaty of Rome and the Single European Act both contain significant measures at encouraging mobility throughout the EC, ensuring that there is no discrimination between Community nationals in their relationships with the state, including education and social security systems. This new provision on citizenship takes those measures a step further.

The scope of the **European Social Fund** is greatly extended beyond the original intentions of job creation in depressed areas: 'to render the employment of workers easier and to increase their geographical and occupational mobility within the Community, and to facilitate their adaptation to industrial changes and to changes in production systems, in particular through vocational training and retraining.'[20] The budget for the ESF has been greatly increased and now offers businesses considerable scope for grants and subsidies for many kinds of job creation, training and relocation programmes. Similar practical assistance from the Community may be gained from new powers of the Community to encourage language training, and the development of distance education.[21] There are also EC funds available to stimulate cooperation on training between educational or training establishments and businesses.

Community legislation on **consumer protection** can now be passed through the Council of Ministers with a qualified majority vote. This means that businesses are likely to face higher levels of consumer protection throughout the Community. One serious problem that arises is the opportunity for individual member states to introduce measures which are more stringent than EC measures which have been adopted in the context of the internal market.[22] There is therefore a danger that exporters may once again be faced with a dozen different sets of regulations which will need to be met trading across the Community.

In order to achieve some of the wider political and economic objectives of European union, there will be a determined programme for the establishment of **trans-European networks** in the areas of transport, telecommunications and energy infrastructures. The treaty makes particular reference to the importance of linking island and peripheral regions with the central regions of the Community. Specific measures such as funding of feasibility studies for trans-European projects, load guarantees or interest rate subsidies will be made available by the Commisssion.

In a move which takes the EC away from its pure free market ideals, the treaty specifies a potentially interventionist role in its relations with **industry**:[23]

- speeding up adjustment of industry to structural changes
- encouraging an environment favourable to initiative and to the development of undertakings throughout the Community, particularly small and medium-sized undertakings
- encouraging an environment favourable to cooperation between undertakings
- fostering better exploitation of the industrial potential of policies of innovation, research and technological development.

Managers should ensure that they remain aware of the various programmes being developed by the European Commission in this area.

Economic and social cohesion rather like the word 'subsidiarity' has had a wide variety of interpretations. For our purposes it is simpler to understand this as attempting to equalize the differences in performance between regions. To this end the structural funds will be particularly directed at rural areas, and the peripheral regions of the Community. The significance of such targeting will be considerable in business location decisions.

Business spending on **research and technological development** is widely accepted as being key to international success, but is also widely acknowledged to be too low. The treaty gives the Community new powers to strengthen the scientific and technological bases of the Community's industry and to encourage it to become more competitive by promoting research activities.[24] Particular focuses will be on technology transfer between the private and public sectors, as well as on cooperation between businesses, especially SMEs.

Environmental policy will, without doubt, be one of the major influences on industrial behaviour in the next decade. The Community has assumed wide powers in this area aimed at:

- preserving, protecting and improving the quality of the environment
- protecting human health
- prudent and rational utilization of natural resources
- promoting measures at international level to deal with regional or worldwide environmental problems

The basis for environmental policy is to aim for a high level of protection. Article 130r also legislates for the first time at an EC level that the polluter should pay. The tensions between the desire for sustainable economic and industrial growth and protection of the environment are likely to cause considerable problems for the Community. At an internal market level, environmental protection is increasingly manifesting itself as a return to the old non-tariff barriers, as individual member states, such as Germany introduce increasingly stringent national environmental legislation before it has been agreed at an international level. Whilst this may not be the expressed intention, it is a clear by-product, and differs little from the old-style barriers to trade. Measures such as the need for all cars to be recycled, or for all manufacturers to accept back for recycling all packaging material will add significantly to industry's costs.

The treaty also lays down the legal basis for fiscal provisions to protect the environment, such as carbon taxes, which will also be a considerable factor in business planning in the future.

The Maastricht Treaty also includes seventeen protocols, and thirty-three declarations, with varying impact. In the main the protocols are binding on their signatories (which may not include all member states), and the declarations are simply statements of policy which seek to clarify the treaty itself. They do remain, however, important. The protocol on **social policy**, for example, from which the UK opted out, significantly extends the provisions for European employment law. The UK opt out may, temporarily, have exempted domestic employers, but any firm planning to have operations in other member states will need to be mindful of the protocol and its implications.

The Treaty on European Union, therefore, extends the scope of the European Community into almost every field of business activity. It is hard to over-estimate its importance. Future development of the Community will certainly continue. Reaction to the treaty, particularly in those countries where ratification was subject to referenda, may have temporarily slowed down some of the excessive ambitions of the EC, but it is already clear that enlargement and widening will proceed. The establishment of the European Economic Area (EEA[25]) is a precursor to the *acquis communautaire* for others. Austria, the Nordic states, Turkey, Israel, and the Central European states are all candidates for accession within the next twenty years. The establishment of the EEA creates a free trade area which will account for 43 per cent of all global trading, and more than 380 million consumers. In general, the EEA agreement extends the single market (but not other aspects of the Community) to the EFTA countries, although border controls will remain. In effect this is a transitional stage to full membership of the Community. For managers in EC member states, however, it opens up significant new markets — and competitive threats. EC rules on freedom of movement of goods, services, labour and capital; competition and environmental policy; company law and public procurement all apply to a greater or lesser extent in EFTA as well as EC countries. Amongst the direct impacts will be the easing of transalpine transport restrictions.

It is not beyond the realms of possibility that the European Community will continue to enlarge to include all of Europe from the Atlantic to the Urals. As well as expanding into the EFTA countries, the Community has also turned its attention to Eastern Europe with a long-term view to some degree of economic integration. Initially the EC's response to the political changes in Eastern Europe has been to provide direct assistance and beneficial external trading arrangements through such programmes as those for Poland and Hungary: assistance for economic restructuring programme (PHARE), which removes quantitative restrictions in specific imports, provides export credits to EC companies trading in those countries, opens up and subsidizes vocational training schemes to Polish and Hungarian nationals, and provides environmental assistance. Parallel programmes are being developed with Bulgaria, Romania and Czechoslovakia. Each programme provides immediate business opportunities for EC companies, as well as useful entrées into these new markets.

Further political developments can be expected, with one, possibly two inter-governmental conferences to debate new treaty amendments already being envisaged before the turn of the century. Uncertainties resulting from the 'petit oui' of the French referendum, and the close rejection, and then adoption by the Danes of the

Maastricht Treaty have already led to special meetings of the Council. Rejection by the Swiss of the EEA, and the changing political colour of many EC member states highlight some of the political divides which exist, and serve as a brake on some of the more idealistic visionaries of a United States of Europe.

The Common Market is very much a political entity. An appreciation of its development, and understanding of its policies is essential for managers developing strategies in this arena. As we can see, this is very much tied in with the management of change. In the next chapter the internal market is examined in some detail, and some general management themes explored.

3 The three free movements

The European Community has now adopted a role which encompasses much more than that of an internal market. As well as the moves towards common defence and foreign policies, there are policies and initiatives aimed at protecting the environment, health and safety, consumer protection, quality standards, competition, employment, transport, intellectual property, public purchasing, and research and development. These are all issues which in their own ways will affect businesses in the EC, but for the purposes of this chapter, should be seen as spokes on the wheel of the internal market.

There are essentially two separate aspects to the internal market: free trade and fair competition between member states. This requires the initial removal of obstacles to the free movement of people, goods, and services, and of certain forms of government interference which led to unfair competition, such as subsidy, and divergent legislation and technical standards. Achievement of the internal market is, as discussed in Chapter 1, an inherent factor in an efficient international trading system. In practice the benefits are various. Stimulating cross-border trade would:

- increase overall levels of economic activity;
- allow for economies of scale and promote efficiency;
- through increased competition better serve the consumer;
- drive prices downwards;
- allow concentrations of European industrial activity to be competitive in global markets;
- stimulate specialization.

Further secondary effects include:

- dispersion of wealth throughout the regions;
- speeding up of industrial restructuring;
- promotion of cultural diversity.

In simple economic terms the European Commission estimated that the combined effects of completion of the single market with the medium-term goals of economic and monetary union would:

- increase Community GDP by 4.5 per cent in addition to normal growth patterns

- deflate consumer prices by 6.1 per cent
- improve public finances by 2.2 per cent of GDP
- boost employment by 1.8 million jobs.[26]

Lord Cockfield, then Commissioner for the internal market, identified around 300 separate measures which would help towards achieving the 'level-playing field' and free trade. These non-tariff barriers range from unnecessary paperwork at borders, to different systems and levels of taxation. Somewhere between the two rests the enormous problem of technical standards. These will be examined in further detail in the next chapter; suffice, at the moment, to note that the British Standards Institution certificates more than 10,000 technical standards, whilst the comparable German DIN certificates more than 20,000. Each one of these presents a potential barrier to trade.

Paolo Cecchini estimated that delays at borders in implementing checks and controls on the movement of goods and services were costing the EC between mecus (million ecus) 425 to 830, administration costs (for business) of border controls were costing mecus 7.5. Additionally it was costing governments between five hundred million and a billion ecus, simply to maintain border controls. These physical barriers, customs posts, are the most obvious obstacles to trade. Border controls have been in place for centuries and fulfil a range of purposes principally involved with stopping people or things from getting in (or out) of a country, and collecting taxes. Other subsidiary uses include the collection of trade statistics. The Internal Market White Paper sought to remove the need for customs border posts within the EC. As a group of islands the United Kingdom has a somewhat different experience of borders, perceiving them as being protective rather administrative instruments. Nevertheless, their removal will have a significant impact on individuals and organizations doing business in the European Community. The removal of border controls has proved to be controversial and difficult. On the one hand the UK has insisted that they remain in order to ensure effective security arrangements (a rather difficult argument to pursue as there are few or no border controls between the UK and the Republic of Ireland), and on the other hand France, Germany and the Benelux, and subsequently Spain, Portugal and Italy following an agreement at Schengen, have jumped the gun and have now nearly completed the abolition of internal borders. (To what extent this will materialize in practice depends to a large extent on the willingness of local police forces.)

The impacts will clearly differ from company to company. Obvious cost reductions will result from factors such as lorries spending less out-time waiting at borders. Other cost reductions will result from the freedom from form-filling. The introduction of the single administrative document which accompanied any goods across borders was a considerable step forward. Its final abolition however, results

Table 3.1   *Removal of physical barriers*

- Simplification of Community transit procedures
- Elimination of customs formalities in the framework of the TIR convention
- Abolition of customs presentation charges
- Duty-free admission of fuel in fuel tanks of coaches and lorries
- Collection of trade statistics
- Transport of dangerous wastes

in the disappearance of more than 60 million forms. Specific regulations easing or removing border formalities have been introduced.

The complete abolition of all customs posts remains elusive and contentious. Some national governments continue to argue that they remain vital to counter the threats of terrorism and drugs. These arguments are becoming decreasingly sustainable in the face of modern policing methods. One complication that will remain for the UK is the inability to distinguish between EC and non-EC goods and people entering the UK at either air or sea ports, necessitating the continuing existence of some forms of control. Nevertheless, the more straightforward aspects of easing the passage across borders are in place. To take a simple example, the abolition of duty on fuel carried in tanks, removes not so much the cost of the duty, but the excessive time taken to measure the fuel in each lorry, before assessing the actual level of duty. For a lorry transporting goods between say Italy and Scotland, these could mean passing across three or four borders, with delays of several hours at each. The savings for exporters and importers are already being enjoyed, and should be benefitting consumers. Unhampered by these additional costs, competition from overseas moves onto at least a slightly less uneven playing field. The lack of border controls also means that distribution strategies should now reflect commercial and economic imperatives rather than artificial and bureaucratic ones. It may, for example, be appropriate for a Scottish company to serve the south-east of England from a distribution centre in Northern France, rather than from Scotland, an option which was not commercially feasible before the border controls were removed.

Much of the nature of removal of border controls has been one of extending the borders to the periphery of the Community. Controls on the import and export of goods into the EC remain high and essential particularly for health and safety reasons.

Many of the 300 pieces of legislation in the Internal Market White Paper are directed at agricultural, veterinary and phytosanitary controls. The necessity of controls in these areas is sometimes questionable, and have in the past proved to be considerable obstacles to trade. Effectively wielded, a health and safety standard can efficiently protect a home industry. For many years, the UK standards on milk were designed, not so much to protect consumers, but more to prevent the import of French UHT milk. Moving the controls to the periphery has required agreement within the Community on the necessary minimum standards within the EC.

Whilst the chances of agreement on contentious policies such as immigration remain elusive, the internal market programme has significantly improved the ability of individuals to cross borders unhindered. The impact on the labour market will be examined in more detail in Chapter 9. Nevertheless, the initiatives have lessened the inconvenience for business travellers. With an increase in export and import activity, businesses will naturally be increasing their physical presence overseas. The simple trip to another member state to visit a potential customer, or to a trade fair, was made difficult through the controls on the movement of individuals, particularly when − as a businessman would be − carrying samples.

Whilst the existence of physical barriers to movement have been the most visible, technical barriers have been the most pervasive and inhibiting. By imposing different technical standards, often under the cloak of health and safety or consumer protection, on goods and products, indigenous industries have been well protected from international competition. This is particularly so in the food manufacturing industry, but also in most others. Exporters have been frustrated in their aims to expand into foreign markets by the need to conform to differing standards. In practice this has often proved to be a sufficient deterrent not to bother. In commercial terms, it may not have proved worth the expense of changing a production line, however slightly, so that a product will conform with the relevant regulations in another member state, let alone in all twelve member states where regulations may even be contradictory. For many years, for example, margarine in Belgium had to be packaged in cubes, rather than tubs. Through the processes of harmonization, approximation and mutual recognition many of these barriers have been removed. If a business is in a sector which has been directly targeted for the removal of technical barriers then the impacts will be considerable, requiring the knowledge and conformance with the EC standards by that business and its competitors.

The immediate impacts are clear: access to wider markets, and greater competition at home. Secondary impacts include the ability to enter into joint ventures, compatibility with ancillary industries, and longevity of product design. Additionally entrance costs into new markets should be lower, with the risks minimized. The wider impact, of course, will be felt by consumers of those products, who will benefit from greater choice from a wider number of producers and distributors.

Fiscal barriers to trade have proved to be harder to remove, and revolve around the distorting impacts of different regimes for VAT and excise duties. The internal market white paper includes twenty-four proposals for ameliorating the situation, particularly aimed to discouraging opportunist cross-frontier purchasing resulting from

Table 3.2   Control of individuals

- Allowances in intra-Community travel
- Tax relief on importation of small consignments of goods of a non-commercial character
- Exemption from VAT on final importation of small consignments of goods
- Easing of controls at intra-Community borders
- Tax exemptions on removals of personal property
- Temporary import of motor vehicles

different VAT rates between member states. VAT plays such an important part of modern business that it is worth spending some time examining how the new EC VAT regime will be implemented, and its effects on businesses and the European economy. Enquiries relating to the new VAT regime are amongst the most frequent put to European information centres.

Value added tax is an integral part of the European Community, and a significant component of business life, particularly in terms of compliance costs. The EC's budget is fixed as a proportion of VAT receipts, and readers will remember its introduction in the UK upon accession to the Community, replacing purchase tax. As has already been examined, fiscal obstacles, as well as the majority of physical obstacles to trade within the Community are being removed. A significant aspect is the new regime for VAT, which will have an impact at a practical level: less paperwork. The European Commission estimates that the new VAT system replaces some 60 million customs documents. At an economic level the removal of fiscal barriers will also stimulate price convergence as retailers will to a much lesser degree be able to mask price differentials behind differences in local taxes.

The extent to which divergent systems and levels of taxation

Table 3.3   Removal of technical barriers

- Simple pressure vehicles
- Safety of toys
- Electromagnetic compatibility
- Machine safety
- Personal protective devices
- Gas appliances
- Electro-medical implantables
- Metrology
- Motor vehicles
- Agricultural machines
- Food
- Pharmaceuticals
- Chemical products
- Construction products

actually distort trade is an issue of some considerable debate. Large and open trading areas such as the United States still manage to enjoy free and fair competition between companies in different states even though there are varying levels of purchase taxes. The European Commission, however, has successfully argued that with the effective removal of customs at frontiers within the EC, and ever improving transport networks, the opportunities for trans-frontier purchasing will increase, and that trading patterns would be distorted, especially across borders between member states where VAT rates were very high and very low. As an island, the United Kingdom has, to a large extent been protected from this type of institutional or structural competition; nevertheless the threat remains.

The 'level playing field' is, of course, a notion that will never be achieved completely, and simply bringing rates of indirect taxation into some sort of line, will not eradicate the price differentials which are beyond the control of businesses: energy costs (where subsidized by the state), corporation tax levels, social security and other employment costs. Whilst consideration has been given to Community-level action in these areas,[27] progress is unlikely in the medium term.

Successful selling in wide sophisticated markets is a complex affair determined by a number of factors, but essentially revolves around the right product of an appropriate quality, delivered at the right time to the right people. And then there is the question of price. No matter how cheap a particular good or service is, if it does not meet the essential requirements it will not sell, but price remains an important factor in the competitive equation. A significant constituent of the price of goods and services is the indirect tax borne by the consumer, either through duties or value added tax.

As cross-border trade increases significant price differentials resulting from differences in indirect taxation would prove to be a major distortion of competition. Price differentials do not have to be so very large to encourage cross-border purchasing, as British day-trippers to France know only too well. A complete harmonization of indirect taxation is clearly unnecessary, as the differences in VAT rates need to be fairly notable to influence consumer spending patterns, but with improved transport links, and easier access to suppliers a wide divergence in VAT rates is incompatible with the notion of an internal market. Approximation to a degree where cross-border shopping does not reap an artificial price advantage is a prerequisite of fair competition. Traders and consumers alike will enjoy considerable benefits from this new agreement which will stimulate intra-Community trade and competition.

Price differentials will remain a significant element in the competitive strategy of companies operating in the single European market. Even large companies, such as Philips, display a wide range of prices for the same product on sale in different countries, which may encourage cross-border purchasing. Businesses considering employing such strategies should, however, be aware of the elements of EC competition policy which are designed to prevent firms from protecting such differentials through anti-competitive and restrictive agreements or practices in relation to distribution.

The new VAT regime[28] is aimed not only at the liberalization of intra-Community trade, but also to relieve a considerable burden of red-tape on traders. It should be borne in mind that this is a transitional regime, designed to last only until 1 January 1997. In brief, the scheme is such that cross-frontier sales between most businesses will be taxed in the hands of the purchaser in the country of destination of goods.[29] After 1996 intra-business sales will be taxed at the seller's end in the country of origin. This has direct implications for form-filling, but also indirect implications for businesses on pricing, as well on governments for the collection of VAT receipts.

There are three basic types of transaction:

1 sales from business to business
2 sales to operators not liable for VAT
3 sales to individuals.

The seller exempts supplies he makes to customers in other member states, thus the responsibility is on the purchaser to advise the seller of his VAT number. The seller makes his normal VAT return which includes notification of the VAT numbers of exempted intra-EC sales. On a quarterly basis there is a requirement to make a return detailing customers, their VAT numbers, and the total value of sales. Invoices must show both the VAT numbers of both seller and purchaser.

The purchaser charges VAT on his purchase as an acquisition. This needs to be declared on the normal VAT return, and can be deducted on the same. With regard to the acquisition, the basic rule is that a sale of goods across borders gives rise to a corresponding acquisition. The tax must be declared in the member state of the acquisition. In the vast majority of cases there will be no charge or a zero charge in the VAT treatment of services between member states, notably in such cases as management consultancy or legal services. Individuals travelling from one member state to another to buy goods will pay VAT where they buy goods, but will not be liable to VAT when they return to their own member state. Duty and tax free sales will continue, within reasonable limits for personal consumption, at ports and airports for intra-Community travel at least until 30 June 1999.

To take a typical example of cross-border trade to show the simplification of paperwork: currently a company selling goods valued at 1,000 ecus for example, across a Community border needs to complete a customs export document for fiscal purposes for each consignment which contains no less than 64 boxes, and complete up to eight copies, submit the document to customs at the customs export office, present the goods for examination on request, issue an invoice, retain the customs documentation and commercial documentation as a proof of export, and include the sale in his VAT return. The buyer then needs to complete customs and import declarations, submit the documentation to customs at the customs import office, present the goods on request, pay or guarantee the VAT, keep the documentation as proof of payment, declare the importation and claim the VAT deduction in his next VAT return. Now that this agreement has been reached the position of international traders is greatly simplified: the seller simply obtains the customer's VAT number, issues an invoice, itemizes the sale in his quarterly return, and includes it in his VAT return. The buyer simply has to keep the commercial documentation, and declare the purchase in his VAT return as a simultaneous debit and credit. The benefits of such simplification cannot be understated.

Other forms of taxation are also attracting the attention of the European Commission in their battle against unfair competition. Taxation is a significant component in the cost-profit equation for all companies, and will have a not inconsiderable impact on, for example, locational decisions. Having addressed indirect taxes, such as VAT and excise duties, there remains the question of corporation taxes. So far, the Community has only tackled some of the peripheral taxation issues, rather than the heart of corporation tax rates. Questions of sovereignty loom large, and inhibit the Community from harmonizing or even approximating corporation taxes. The Internal Market programme does, however address some of the anomalies which have inhibited cross-border cooperation, and expansion into other member states. Directives covering double taxation, tax regimes for international parents and subsidiaries, taxation of mergers, and carryover of losses are now all in place, and need to be borne in mind. In general they have contributed to easing the complications for corporations seeking to operate in more than one member state. Nevertheless the distortions, particularly in costs, arising from corporation taxes, both national and local, remain.

Issues of public procurement, new technologies, company law, and intellectual property will be considered in later chapters. However, within the realm of freedom of movement, remains the pressing question of free movement of capital. Financial services are, of course, an important sector, which required an injection of competition. More importantly though, for managers in industry and commerce will be the effect of having a complete single market in financial services. All organizations have some need for financial services, ranging from banking and insurance to transactions in securities.

European law now provides a comprehensive framework for the financial services, which should ensure greater choice and compe-

Table 3.4   Common market for financial services

- Bank accounts
- Foreign bank accounts
- Solvency ratios
- Mortgage credit
- Credit insurance
- Motor insurance
- Life insurance
- Public equity issues
- Investment services

tition between providers in an increasingly complex marketplace. New forms and sources of credit, for example, benefiting from perhaps lower interest rates in other countries are becoming available to business which can be used with a higher degree of confidence by the customer.

The other major ancillary service enjoyed by businesses, which contributes to the free movement of goods, services and people, is the liberalization of the transport sector, which again should have the effect of reducing prices, improving competition between carriers, and simplifying transport procedures. By freeing carriers from unnecessary restrictions – such as bans on cabotage, exporters will be able to move goods about the Community more efficiently, and benefit from the abolition of unfair or monopolistic practices.

Further, more specific parts of the internal market programme designed to assist business include the opening up of public procurement markets, liberalization of telecommunications and postal services, development of EC intellectual property law, as well as measures to improve labour mobility, restrict state aids, and industrial, environmental and regional policies. These will all be covered in later chapters. The essence of the single market remains the three free movements.

There will be no business or individual within the European Community unaffected by the establishment of the single market. Nevertheless it is important to remember that this is only the start of a long-term vision for European integration and union, where, as in any process of restructuring there will be individual winners and losers. The gains to the Community as a whole will be achieved at the cost of whole sectors of the economy. Organizations seeking to benefit will need to consider carefully their own location, size, products, structures, practices and philosophies in the face of this turbulent change.

The essence of the single market is the ability for companies in Bradford to be able to trade as easily in Bristol, as in Barcelona, and vice versa, and thus encourage greater and fairer competition. For individual companies this requires an understanding of the market segmentations that are likely to be developed. Careful consideration will need to be given to what strategies will be appropriate to expansion in new markets, and to how best to defend existing markets. The effects of economic clustering will need to be clearly understood by each company. Management practices and corporate structures will need to be reviewed to see whether they match the new needs for scale of operation, specialization and flexibility. Different skills in the labour force will be essential to survival and success. New opportunities are likely to be presented for some businesses through specific sectoral programmes. All of this will put considerable pressure on the quality of management, and these are just the results of implementation of a White Paper in 1985.

Wider pressures will be brought to bear on the generality of the management community, as well as specifically on certain sectors. Competition law at Community level will prove increasingly effective (and intrusive) in controlling the operations of businesses and their competitors. Progressive abolition of state aids will be immediately detrimental to current recipients, but of considerable benefit to their competitors. In the same vein, the internal market will implicitly lead to the withdrawal of state monopolies in many sectors, including energy, water and telecommunications. Specific programmes for SMEs, for technological innovation, for trade with Eastern Europe and the Mediterranean countries will present new opportunities.

From a wider perspective, the single European market, and its future development is not simply a factor to be taken into consideration, but the whole environment in which managers will have to manage. '1992' was cited by only one in five respondents to a 1990 BIM survey[30] as very important to them. This is not to minimize the importance, but to underline those challenges which will contribute to success in Europe. The top challenges cited were: making the organization structure more flexible, continuing management education and development, and creating a devolved organization for people.

4 Standards

The removal of technical barriers to trade within the EC and EEA constitutes the major impact on trade flows. As well as creating unacceptable administrative costs, divergent national technical standards on products distort production patterns, increase unit costs, increase stock holding costs, and discourage businesses from cooperation. Whether we look at different shapes for electric plugs, dimensions of white goods, or wavelengths for cellular telephones the lack of common standards inhibits both trade between member states, and also the development of international competitiveness through industrial sectors based on home markets of continental proportions.

The history of standardization in Europe is a long and complex one, with several false dawns. In brief though, it was initially considered appropriate to develop European standards for as many products as possible. Inevitably though the task of harmonizing national standards – often a case of persuading eleven member states to drop their own national standard and conform to that of another – proved to be difficult, and indeed could not keep up with technological developments. By the time a standard had been agreed, the product itself was often out-moded and had been replaced by another. Because the development of European standards has its greatest impact in the initial phases of product development, attempts to harmonize across the Community were unsatisfactory.

There are several reasons for European standardization, not all of which are complementary, and each responding to a different approach to standardization:

- **Preventing barriers to trade within the market**
  Products should not be refused entry into foreign markets simply because they do not conform to what might be an arbitrary national norm; the process of mutual recognition is the appropriate mechanism for overcoming such obstacles, as the erstwhile Belgian margarine standard that required margarine to be packaged in cubes.
- **Encouraging EC-wide cooperation between manufacturers and distributors**
  Common standards of goods allow for compatibility between different goods, distribution and servicing systems. Dishwasher manufacturers in one country, should be able to collaborate with kitchen designers in another confident that their dishwashers will fit under

standard height work-surfaces in kitchens throughout the EC, would be able to be serviced, and indeed could be shipped in a standard manner across Europe. Precise and common standards are required, but should be influenced by the market rather than bureaucrats.

- **Stimulating research and development of new products**
  Large scale research and development projects consuming enormous resources require several national markets in order to recoup costs. Modern digital telephone exchanges, for example, could never have been developed if their sale was restricted to one country. Again common standards are required, but it is inherently difficult to agree standards for products that have yet to be developed, and brought to market, such as high-definition television.

- **Assuring the safety of consumers**
  Many technical standards exist purely to protect consumers or workers and need to be maintained at the highest level. It would clearly be wrong for the Community to ease technical barriers at the price of allowing dangerous or unsafe products onto the market. Broad minimum standards should apply, mutual recognition of national standards and national testing and certification should suffice to assure a high level of consumer protection.

It is now, broadly speaking, illegal for individual member states to set national technical standards which prevent free and fair competition, such as the German behaviour towards foreign lawn-mower imports. Nevertheless, the legal changes need to be reflected in the marketplace. With currently three different types of television broadcasting in the EC (PAL, SECAM and MAC) the development of a global television competitiveness is being severely hampered. Differing standards inhibit the willingness of business to open up new markets for their products. Mutual recognition of minimum standards only allows goods to be marketed, it contributes little to the enablement of marketing. Simply being permitted to sell a product in another country does not mean that product will actually work there or be bought. Managers cannot, therefore be complacent about the development of European standards – particularly electrical standards, and should be involved in the process of standardization.

The failure to agree detailed technical standards at a European level (Euro-norms) brought about the 'New Approach' embodying the principles of mutual recognition laid down in the Cassis de Dijon case. The new approach lays down only the minimum requirements for health and safety, which are defined in standards directives (as well as in consumer and environmental protection legislation), and leaves it to the European standardization bodies CEN, CENELEC and ETSI to develop industrial standards to ensure compatibility. These are then implemented by national standards bodies (BSI, DIN etc.) at a detailed level, often with the aid of sectoral groups, within agreed rules on testing, certification and inspection. One impact of this new approach is some relief from the burden of testing and checking in each member state where products are to be marketed. If products have been tested in accredited testing laboratories, then under the principle of mutual recognition, it is unlikely that rechecking and testing will be required in any other member state.

New approach directives cover an increasingly wide number of areas: toys, simple pressure vehicles, electromagnetic compatibility, machine safety, personal protective equipment, elecro-medical implantables, gas appliances, mobile machines, non automatic weighing machines, and in-vitro diagnostic products.

Additionally, however, there are numerous old approach directives which still need to be conformed with including:

- 22 directives concerned with building and civil engineering equipment
- 2 directives on construction products
- directive on cosmetics products
- directive on crystal glass
- 10 directives on dangerous substances and preparations
- 7 directives on electrical equipment
- 7 directives on fertilizers
- 2 directives on fuels
- 4 directives on gas appliances
- 3 directives on information technology
- 33 directives on metrology
- 3 directives on motor cycles
- 69 directives on motor vehicles
- 2 directives on noise from domestic appliances
- 3 directives on packaging
- 17 directives on pharmaceuticals
- 7 directives on telecommunications
- 3 directives on television
- 8 directives on textiles
- 2 directives on tobacco
- 44 directives on tractors and agricultural machinery
- 3 directives of veterinary products
- 23 directives on foodstuffs
- 24 directives on food additives
- 11 directives on materials in contact with foodstuffs
- 13 directives on packaging of foodstuffs

These European standards are clearly wide ranging, and cover such detailed issues as the size of rear registration plates on cars, through to noise levels of washing machines, radio interference from electrical goods, content of mineral water or cosmetics. Proposals for EC standards often give rise to ill-informed comment in national newspapers, about the EC trying to ban certain products. It is rarely the case that this is true. The establishment of technical standards is enabling rather than restrictive, but needs to take account of high levels of consumer protection. So, when the European Commission seeks to define the minimum content of cocoa in a bar of chocolate, it is trying to open up the markets, not to prevent the sale of sweets. The involvement of industry in the process of standardization is vital. European Commission officials are limited in their knowledge and will make genuine mistakes. In 1991 there was a considerable outcry in the press following the publication of a proposal on food additives which appeared to ban flavoured crisps. The heat generated by the 'prawn-cocktail crisps' debate, obscured the fact that neither crisp manufacturers nor the UK government had been monitoring the progress of the proposal, and failed to alert the Commission to the prevalent manufacturing processes for crisps in the UK.

The list of products likely to be affected by European standardization is therefore extensive and likely to impact on most parts of industry. In the near future proposals are expected on lifts, pressure containing equipment, fairground and playground equipment, recreational craft and second-hand machinery. Few, if any, products will not be covered by European standards. Managers need to be aware of their existence, and involved in their development. Not only to ensure compliance (which could mean survival if your product does not meet a new standard), but also to be aware of the opportunities presented for collaboration, new markets, and cooperation. Products which conform with the new approach directives must carry the EC kitemark. Detailed information on each relevant standard can be obtained from the British Standards Institution.

Many non-binding but nevertheless vitally important technical standards are being agreed voluntarily at a sectoral level, such as standards for cellular telephones, where competing manufacturers have perceived their common interest in the development of compatible standards to ensure longevity of product life and wide markets. The involvement of firms in their relevant trade associations, especially at a European level will become increasingly important if companies are to be aware of the fast-changing standards, and to be able to influence them. In line with the political nature of the European Community, there are inevitable struggles over the agreement of technical standards, with each national industry seeking to assure the pre-eminence of its own standard as the European standard, in order to avoid expensive adaptation. The British, German and Italian standards bodies have been the most effective in pushing their own standards, particularly the latter, less through having efficient standards, but by the active participation of practising managers in the working parties and committees of CEN.

One further standards issue that should be considered by all managers operating in the single market, is that of quality assurance. According to Sir Derek Hornby, quality management is 'likely to be the single most important factor in determining how effectively

British companies meet the challenge of Europe.[31] In the UK this means conforming with British Standard BS5750, which is comparable with the relevant European and international standards EN29000 and ISO9000. Not only will this provide a system of effective quality control and management, but it is also a useful marketing tool to increasingly sophisticated consumers operating in a marketplace with wider choice but fewer differentiators. BS5750 requires the establishment of a quality management policy with clear responsibilities within the organization for documenting, and identifying, remedying and preventing recurrences of defects. The attainment of a recognized quality management standard is also important in bidding for public sector contracts. These will be dealt with in some detail in Chapter 11, but it is worth bearing in mind at this point, that whilst public sector bodies are no longer allowed to discriminate on grounds of nationality, they may, and increasingly will, insist that contractors have BS5750 or its equivalent.

5 Economic and Monetary Union

Probably the most significant development in the European Community's history is the move towards economic and monetary union. The implications for business will be widespread, ranging from large macro-economic questions relating to regional economic divergence and interest rate policies, through to the costs of changing money, and comparative pricing levels.

The economies of EC member states have become increasingly integrated – their trade with each other account for more than 50 per cent of their total external trade. Additionally, a number of factors (such as increased capital mobility resulting in speculative flows of foreign exchange) show that movement in exchange rates was not necessarily a direct reflection of a country's balance of trade and the movement of goods across its borders. A simple comparison of purchasing parity with nominal exchange rates amply demonstrates the inability of modern currencies to reflect comparative advantage. Exchange rates have become increasingly disconnected from the state of a country's economy, and less and less fulfil the role of money, and more of a commodity, reflecting only the risk of devaluation and the premia of interest rates.

Political commitment to EMU across the wider Community was contained in the Single European Act: 'The Heads of State ... approved the objective of the progressive realization of Economic and Monetary Union.' It is finally embodied in the Treaty on European Union.

The history of the EMU really starts in July 1944 at a conference in Bretton Woods, held to examine problems of international payments. Among other initiatives the conference laid the groundwork for the establishment of the International Monetary Fund (IMF). In 1969 the six EC member states committed themselves to the principles of achieving economic and monetary union. The Werner Report (1970) established an initial framework for this with two guiding principles:

- that there should be a single EEC currency (or at least the total convertibility of European currencies and irreversible fixing of their exchange rates, which amounts to much the same thing);
- that some responsibilities for monetary and credit policy, presently with national governments, should be transferred to the Community level.

The initial implementation of the Werner report became known as

'The Snake'. This developed into the European Monetary system (EMS), of which the Exchange Rate Mechanism (ERM) is an integral part. EMS is one stage towards EMU.

The European Council in Brussels which agreed on 4 and 5 December 1978 to set up the EMS made the following statement as to its purpose:

> The purpose of the European Monetary System is to establish a greater measure of monetary stability in the Community. It should be seen as a fundamental component of a more comprehensive strategy aimed at a lasting growth with stability, a progressive return to full employment, the harmonization of living standards and the lessening of regional disparities in the Community. The European Monetary System will facilitate the convergence of economic development and give fresh impetus to the process of European Union. The Council expects the European Monetary System to have a stabilizing effect on international economic and monetary relations. It will therefore be in the interests of the industrialized and the developing countries alike.[32]

The European Currency Unit (ECU) is the central tool of the EMS. It is a basket currency, the composition of which is supposed to reflect the economic strength of each of the Community's member states. The calculation of the weights applied to its composition takes into account each country's gross domestic product, its participation in the Community's external trade and its quotas under the short-term monetary support system.

The ecu is now being used in a number of different forms, particularly for private transactions and with increasing sophistication on the world's capital markets. However, within the ERM it fulfils four basic functions:

- As the denominator of the Exchange Rate Mechanism (ERM); a central rate expressed in ecus is fixed for each currency in the EMS. (For countries which do not participate in the ERM this is a purely theoretical rate.) From these central rates a grid of bilateral exchange rates and fluctuation margins are calculated.
- As the basis for the divergence indicator of the ERM; this indicator acts as a sort of early-warning device to identify any currency which is diverging from the average for the other currencies. Unlike movement against just one currency, this shows when a currency is diverging from the other members as a whole. Members are obliged to formulate (and adjust if necessary) their economic and monetary policies to ensure that this divergence does not happen. This function is key to the role of the EMS in encouraging the convergence of EC members' policies.
- As the denominator for operations within the ERM; operations within the ERM include both intervention and credit mechanisms. These are denominated in ecus.
- As a reserve instrument and a means of settlement among central

banks; in its role as a reserve instrument, the ecu is issued by the European Monetary Cooperation Fund (EMCF) to the EMS central banks, in exchange for deposits by them of 20 per cent of the gold and dollar reserves. The amount of ecu created as a result is adjusted every three months to take into account changes in the level of gold and dollar reserves and of variations in the ecu price of these assets. Outside of EMS, the ecu has started to fulfil a number of separate roles, as a prototype European currency:

- It is already in widespread use in the financial markets, particularly through the issues of ecu bonds, and gilts;
- Trading contracts are increasingly (although still a small fraction of all contracts) negotiated and struck in ecus;
- Attempts have been made by the Belgian Government to issue ecu traveller's cheques, which are understood to be accepted quite widely throughout Europe. In its zeal the Belgian government has even gone as far as to mint ecu coins which, on an experimental basis, were accepted by restaurants, hotels and taxis in Brussels for a short time.

There are two basic rules which define the ERM: respect of the fluctuation margins and realignments by common accord, the purose of which is to ensure confidence in the different currencies, and the sound economic management of each member state. As described above, bilateral central rates are calculated to express the rates between all currencies within the EMS. For those participating in the ERM a margin is allowed to limit movement by currencies against their bilateral central rates. These fluctuation margins provide 'floor' and 'ceiling' rates within which central banks are obliged to maintain their currencies. This is achieved by intervening on the money markets to influence the exchange rate by expanding or reducing supply. The central bank of the country with the strong currency buys the weak currency, and the central bank of the country with the weak currency sells the strong currency. The obligation to do this is binding and there is no maximum limit to the amount of currency which a central bank is required to buy or sell to maintain the system. It is recognized that central bank intervention has very little real impact on the global flows of currency. However, it does provide a very clear signal to the money markets that a bank (or government) is determined, through its monetary policy, to maintain a value for that currency.

EMS realignments can only take place with common accord. This is a major difference between EMS and its predecessors, the Snake and Bretton Woods, where realignments were effectively decided unilaterally. Common accord for realignments reinforces the credibility of the system as speculators are left in no doubt that central banks will be committed to intervention if necessary.

Additionally, it acts as a safeguard against members attempting to devalue their currencies as a competitive act. Proponents of EMS argue that this is the major strength of the EMS, and will encourage national economies, industry, and even individual pay negotiators to behave responsibly and efficiently once deprived of the crutch of devaluation.

EMS should be seen as stage 1 of Economic and Monetary Union, which should be complete once Greece joins the ERM, and the UK, Portugal and Spain move into the narrow bands. Stage 2 is timetabled but unlikely to commence on 1 January 1994 at which time a European Monetary Institute (EMI) shall commence its operations. Its role will be to strengthen cooperation between central banks, coordinate monetary policies, promote the efficiency of cross-border payments, and prepare the rules of operation for stage 3. This transitional phase is likely to be one of considerable political and economic turbulence, with major stresses occurring at national, regional and corporate levels, as individual currencies are manoeuvred into position for stage three, and local economies struggle to converge. At a national level, the governments of member states are required to bring down their levels of deficit to 3 per cent of GDP and overall debt to 60 per cent of GDP.[33]

If by the end of 1997 the date for the beginning of the third stage has not been set, the third stage will begin on 1 January 1999 provided that a majority of member states fulfil the necessary conditions for the adoption of a single currency. The measures by which this decision will be made are the rate of inflation, government deficit, history of fluctuation within ERM, and interest rate levels. As has been discussed, the susceptibility of politicians to electorally expedient manipulation of currencies can be strong. Nevertheless, the agreed intentions that underlie stage 2 are for convergence at the lowest possible level. Managers should therefore be preparing their options for medium-term strategies with low interest rates, low inflation, and a stable currency in mind. The short-term benefits enjoyed by UK businesses from successive devaluations of sterling are likely to be rare, and transitory (as others follow similar policies of competitive devaluations, which only lead to bouts of inflation), and should not be relied upon to achieve competitiveness in the single market.

Economic convergence of national economies − let alone regional economies, by the end of the century is an ambitious project, and stage 3 is unlikely to be achieved simultaneously. In all probability the majority of member states will move to irrevocably fixed exchange rates, and then to a single currency and will be followed by the rest over several years. The UK's own move to stage 3 will require the assent of the parliament of the day. The significant point about this structure is that one member state will not be able to prevent the others from forming a monetary union within the European Community. Stage 2 and the initial years of stage 3 are likely to leave UK managers at something of a disadvantage compared to those of more convergent economies.

Once the move to stage 3 has been reached, the ecu will become a currency in its own right. Some member states may give up their own currencies, but others will simply fix their exchange rates to the ecu. The European Central Bank (ECB) or the EMI will have sole responsibility for issuing notes and coins, whilst monetary policy will be the responsibility of the European System of Central Banks who will have the over-riding task of maintaining price stability – very much in the manner of the existing German Bundesbank.

Exchange rate fixity and economic convergence will have a variety of direct effects on UK businesses:

- Pricing transparency throughout the Community will put downward pressure on prices.
- Lower costs of finance will result from freeing of capital markets, but also from the pressures to reduce interest rates throughout the Community on the back of low levels of inflation. In the meantime, however, *real* interest rates are likely to remain high for some time.
- Pricing confidence arises from the removal of risk of currency volatility.
- Exchange costs will be minimized. Using the ecu for both purchasing and selling will allow for a fairer comparison of prices. Furthermore the costs of transferring money from one currency to another will be removed. For SMEs this has been a significant cost of doing business overseas. For larger companies the costs of large foreign exchange treasury operations may be reduced – these have, however, in some cases been generators of large profits which will also be removed.

Economic and Monetary Union could, therefore, be seen by managers as simply the removal of further obstacles to trade. But the elimination of exchange rate variability, uncertainty and transaction costs are only part of the effect. During both stage 2 and 3, the economic and monetary policies which will be pursued by national authorities and the Community bodies will be single-mindedly directed towards the goal of price stability, perhaps ignoring the particular needs of differently performing regions or countries. EMU is intrinsically deflationary and moves towards economic conver-

Table 5.1 Benefits of European Economic and Monetary Union

- *Efficiency and growth*
- *Price stability*
- *Public finances*
- *Employment and regional balance*
- *Equity*

gence may result in inappropriate economic policies being pursued in countries requiring reflationary measures. Regions enjoying strong growth will require very different economic conditions to those regions in recession, and there will need to be balancing mechanisms, principally through the structural funds to ensure that poorly performing regions are not effectively strangled by the economic measures being used against high performing regions. Low performing regions will be competing at an economic disadvantage in their need to attract capital and human resource, and are likely to seek higher rates of public expenditure and lower interest rates. In essence this is a balance of payments problem on a regional scale.

With the removal of different currencies as the final obstacle to freedom of movement there will remain only artificial mechanisms to encourage or discourage economic clustering, including employment costs, fiscal advantages, subsidies, and regulation.

6 Competition

Michael Porter begins his book *The Competitive Advantage of Nations*[34] with the question 'Why do some social groups, economic institutions, and nations advance and prosper?' He notes that the study of the question is a study of competitiveness, which means many different things to different people: 'To firms, competitiveness meant the ability to compete in world markets with a global strategy. To many members of Congress, competitiveness meant that the nation had a positive balance of trade. To some economists, competitiveness meant a low unit cost of labour adjusted for exchange rates.'[35]

Competition policy is the guiding light for the European Community. Not surprisingly it is the area where the European Commission has the most direct power over business, able to intervene of its own initiative to prevent anti-competitive practices, in its attempts to provide a framework for both free and fair competition throughout the EC. The implications are widespread, and policies in this area cover 'the level-playing field'; mergers, acquisitions and monopolies; restrictive trade practices; barriers to entry; dumping; and state aids and subsidies.

Broadly speaking the basis of the level playing fields lies in Article 100 of the Treaty which gives the Commission the power to issue directives for the approximation of laws, regulations and administrative provisions of the member states such as directly affect the establishment or functioning of the common market. This power is sufficiently broad to have given rise to considerable concern about the competence of the Community to act in a number of areas. The Commission has taken the view that it should act wherever there is a potential distortion of competition. Article 100 has been used controversially as the basis for legislation in a number of fields including employment law.

The level playing field as a concept reflects the notion that all individuals and businesses should be able to compete on equal terms with each other, without hindrance from differing regulations. The Commission has therefore attempted to harmonize as many areas as possible. It remains, however, a futile and indeed paradoxical task. If the principle of comparative advantage is accepted, then the competitiveness of EC industries may be damaged by a levelling out of regulatory conditions.

The Commission has, for example, taken the view that divergent employment conditions are distorting competition. Employment laws should, therefore, be approximated so that a business in one member state does not manage to have a competitive advantage because, say, rates of maternity pay are less, or health and safety regimes are less stringent and therefore costly. The ability to level out the competitive playing field is, of course, limited. The competitiveness of business is determined not only by the regulatory framework, but other factors such as access to distribution networks, availability of skilled labour, raw materials and even climate and hours of daylight. Nevertheless, as a broad principle of Community policy all businesses should be able to benefit from an EC regime which seeks to ensure that no company should be at a disadvantage because its compliance with its national legislation is more costly than for its competitors.

As has been mentioned there remains a dichotomy between the level playing field and the principle of subsidiarity, which we see emerging particularly in the fields of environmental and consumer protection legislation, and manifesting itself in opt-outs. It therefore remains doubtful that the Commission will ever succeed in creating a truly level playing field. Managers cannot therefore assume that regulatory conditions in one part of the Community will be equal to those of another, but they are likely to approximate.

One of the fundamental pillars of any competition policy is the way in which it treats monopolies, particularly those arrived at by the process of merger and acquisition. From a broad policy perspective there will always be a tension within a trading bloc such as the EC between, on the one hand, the need to ensure fair competition within the trading bloc, which means breaking up monopolies or companies in a dominant position within the territory, and on the other hand, the need to allow companies to come together on a sufficient scale to be able to compete effectively in global markets.

Merger and acquisition are among the most common strategies being adopted by EC companies to break into new markets. The process of merger is an efficient mechanism which brings with it immediate access to the marketplace, new products, skills, local knowledge etc. The Commission is, rightly, keen to encourage such forms of cooperation, by harmonizing different national provisions in order to simplify the process and indeed open up the process. However, it retains strong powers to prevent abuses, and has the right to vet proposed mergers over a certain size.

The Third Company Law Directive (78/885/EEC) harmonizes national merger and acquisition legislation of public companies. Differing national procedures, and levels of protection for creditors, shareholders and other stakeholders have, in the past, made it more difficult to acquire companies in some member states than others. Inevitably cultures differ across the EC. In the UK pure mergers are rare; the usual practice is acquisition by one dominant party. In Germany, the practice of hostile takeovers − common in the UK, is comparatively rare. The Third Company Law Directive provides a common basis of law in this area, covering such areas as the publication of prospectuses, arrangements for shareholders' meetings, and protection of employees. This therefore eases the process. On the other end of this policy is the 1989 regulation which seeks to inhibit the development of monopolies at a European level. Businesses engaged on strategies of expansion through acquisition need to be mindful of the regulation. Just as a national regulator can refer a proposed merger or acquisition to an arbitrator (in the UK the Office of Fair Trading, and the Monopolies and Mergers Commission) to test whether or not a merger is in the public interest, the European Commission retains the right to perform a similar task at Community level. In practice the division between the responsibilities of national regulators and Community regulation is one of size. The 1989 regulation[36] has three criteria (which are due to be revised in 1993/4):

1　a threshold of combined world sales of more than 5 billion ecus;
2　a threshold of combined EC sales of more than 250 million ecus;
3　the combined group must have more than a third of its sales in a second member state.

If all these criteria are met then the Commission has the right to examine the public interest of the merger for its competitive impact: structure of the market, actual and potential competition, and freedom of choice by consumers, partners and distributors are all taken into account.

Companies involved in such large-scale merger activity are obliged to notify and seek prior clearance from the Commission, which can then suspend the merger for up to four months while it completes its investigations. The regulation removes a considerable degree of uncertainty about where the power to regulate lies, but the delays of a reference to the Commission can be seriously damaging to the merger process, not only involving increased costs, but potentially lost opportunities. Failure to notify in accordance with the regulation can leave companies open to financial penalties of between 1,000 ecus and 50,000 ecus. Failure to notify a concentration and then to go ahead results in fines of up to 10 per cent of a company's turnover. Companies should therefore err on the side of caution when making any kind of cross-border joint arrangement on a large scale. Companies must notify the Commission of an agreement to conduct a joint venture, merger or acquisition within one week of the agreement being reached on a standard form, which should detail the effects of the agreement on the market as a whole. Commercial confidentiality is assured, but the notification is published in the *Official Journal*. The Commission has the power to approve, subject to modifications, reject, or require divestiture of certain parts of the concentration. Its decisions are similarly published in the *Official Journal*. The vast majority of notifications are approved – although most subject to some form of modification, but companies should be wary of the considerable investigative powers of the Commission in this area.

Competition policy is something of a two-edged sword. On the one hand it is restrictive on the sorts of strategies that can be adopted, imposes significant compliance costs and complications, but on the other hand it does the same for your competitors. The basis for competition policy in the Community is Articles 85 and 86 of the treaty which prohibit:

- the direct or indirect fixing of purchase or selling prices or of any other trading conditions
- the limitation or control of production, markets, technical development or investment
- market-sharing or the sharing of sources of supply
- the application to parties to transactions of unequal terms in respect of equivalent supplies, thereby placing them at a competitive disadvantage
- the subjecting of the conclusion of a contract to the acceptance by a party of additional supplies, which either by their nature or according to commercial usage have no connection with the subject of such contract.

Articles 85 and 86 are sufficiently well defined[37] to be directly applicable on all individuals and organizations operating inside the European Community. Managers should also be wary that simple compliance with existing UK competition law does not necessarily provide a defence against contravening EC law if that law has not been adequately transposed by UK legislation. A complete awareness and understanding by all managers of EC law in this area is therefore advisable to avoid a contravention. Competition law is inevitably fraught with political complications and has thus been established by a build-up of case law. However the Articles provide the fundamental basis.

Articles 85 and 86 prohibit price-fixing, and market-sharing, essentially outlawing cartels within the EC. Even such practices as where a supplier seeks to impose a minimum retail resale price on a distributor or retailer are considered to be price-fixing, because they restrict that retailer's ability to set his own policies and carry out his own trade. Companies should be careful about entering into joint sales-promotion agreements, exchanging information with competitors, and even any attempt at coordinating market activity through trade associations. Production or sales limits − such as quotas on right-hand drive cars are similarly illegal. Any agreement which seeks to inhibit what, how much and where a retailer may operate is in contravention of Article 85. If a company has separate agents in each member state, it should not, therefore, seek to restrict one from operating in another area. Restricting supplies to actual or potential distributors is also considered anti-competitive. Companies must therefore be very careful when establishing exclusive distribution arrangements, as these are seen as being barriers to entry into the marketplace. Furthermore it is now doubtful whether a supplier can impose a differential pricing system to retailers in different countries. Any agreement which is in contravention of Article 85 is deemed to be null and void and unenforceable.

In seeking to conform with Articles 85 and 86 companies must not only examine their practices in the horizontal market to see whether they are distorting, or inhibiting competition, but also vertically. An agreement which, for example, gave one chain of shops the right to sell a particular product, may not have a competitive impact between product brands, but does inhibit competition between retailers. A producer of top of the range perfumes, for example, would have difficulties in preventing its sale in stores which it did not believe matched the products' particular image or branding.

The Commission has recognized the tension between the commercial desire to enter into cooperative agreements across the EC, and Article 85, particularly for small and medium-sized companies, and has therefore said that it is unlikely to invoke Article 85 where the turnover of the undertakings is less than 200 million ecus and the agreement involved covers less than 5 per cent of the market share, within the relevant geography.

In recognition of existing arrangements, there are a number of specific regulations which provide a degree of exemption from or clarification of Article 85 in certain areas:

- exclusive distribution agreements (EEC/1983/83), which restrict the types of agreements, for example prohibiting companies from banning parallel imports
- exclusive purchasing agreements for beer and petrol (EEC/1984/83)
- motor vehicle servicing agreements (EEC/1985/125)
- research and development agreements (EEC/1985/418)
- air transport (EEC/1987/3976)
- certain franchising agreements (EEC/89/556) define the types of restrictions which may be imposed by a franchiser. Similar rules govern licensing agreements.

The primary concern of business managers with regard to competition policy is to ensure compliance. An agreement does not have to be in the form of a contract; an informal, even verbal, agreement can still be in contravention of Article 85. However, managers should be mindful of the protection that is afforded by the legislation, and should be alert to competitors acting in contravention of the policies. Most investigations carried out by DG4 are as the result of a tip-off from competitors or aggrieved consumers.

Whilst the EC goes to considerable lengths to protect consumers from anti-competitive practices within the Community, it does also provide EC commerce and industry with some degree of protection from anti-competitive behaviour from non-EC companies, particularly from dumping.[38] The Community's anti-dumping policies are closely tied to the GATT agreements. Nevertheless an industry which is competing against subsidized imports, or dumped goods does have recourse to legal protection and redress in the form of tariffs. Dumping is illegal within the Community, and the GATT treaties allow for the imposition of anti-dumping tariffs to be imposed, or undertakings of price increases to be enforced. Recent cases have involved the import of dot-matrix printers from Japan, where a countervailing duty has been imposed. Other cases have covered imports of audio tapes, radios, and paper.

It is rarely easy to prove that dumping is going on, and in practice it is difficult for a single company to make the case, as detailed information about domestic and global markets need to be put forward. If the case is put that an import has benefited from subsidy this is generally even harder to prove, as this may cover preferential loans, regional aids, R & D support programmes, transport subsidies etc., some of which are permitted, some not. Injury to the domestic industry must also be proved. If a company suspects that a non-EC competitor is dumping goods in the domestic market this should be raised with the relevant trade association who can act on that company's behalf. Investigations can take years to carry out, so provisional duties may be imposed if there is a prima facie case of dumping.

Dumping is a very grey area within competition policy, and one that is politically charged. Accusations of protectionism, and fortress Europe are often heard whenever anti-dumping measures are taken. On the face of it it does not appear to be in the consumers' interests for the Commission to be forcing up prices of particular commodities so as to remove an aggressive competitive market entry from a non-EC manufacturer. Nevertheless, the policies do provide some degree of protection (of questionable benefit) for indigenous industries. The issue is further complicated by the establishment of foreign owned 'screwdriver' assembly plants, particularly in the United Kingdom.

Within the European Community individual companies also benefit from protection against unfair competition derived from state aids and subsidies. In general articles 91–93 of the Treaty of Rome prohibit most forms of state aids. Removing barriers to entry into new markets will not be sufficient to stimulate competition unless all parties are operating on an equal basis. Ironically it has been the very removal of barriers to competition which has led to greater calls for protection from beleaguered industrial sectors. Most forms of protection being outlawed, the temptation has been a recourse to subsidy and assistance from the state. Article 92 covers all forms of aid which threatens to distort competition between member states. Levels of subsidy have changed little since 1981, but the pressure from the Commission, and the increasing willingness to use its powers in this area are certain to further lower levels of state aid,

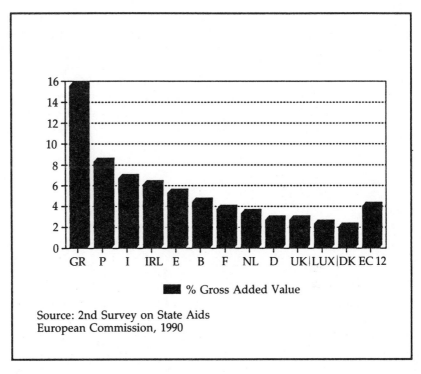

Figure 6.1 *Aids to manufacturing industry*

particularly in countries such as Greece and Portugal. All this will be of direct benefit to new market entrants, and to industries which have managed to survive and be competitive without assistance. Those who have been reliant on state aids for years now find themselves weak and vulnerable. This presents a significant opportunity for strong and competitive companies to establish new market share.

State aids can take many forms, including grants, tax reductions or deferrals, equity participation, soft loans, and guarantees. These are generally of a direct or vertical nature. State aids which are horizontal or general, are permitted in certain circumstances, and include government interventions in innovation, the environment, SMEs, export promotion, energy efficiency, training and unemployment. The distinction between direct and general aids is not a clear one. It is, for example, permissible for industry to receive grants to be more energy efficient, but illegal for it to benefit from subsidized electricity. SMEs[39] benefit from a more relaxed regime, and the state may provide low-interest loans to new businesses, and grants for research and development.

Significantly this is one area where the Commission has greater powers than the Council of Ministers. It has the authority to enforce changes to specific government aids, including repayments of subsidy — as happened during the Rover sell-off to British Aerospace. Managers need therefore to be very wary of accepting most forms of assistance from the state — which includes local authorities. Simply because it is made available does not mean that it is legal under the treaty, and the Commission has the power to review all forms of state aid. This should be used to the advantage of companies who may complain to the European Commission if they feel that a competitor is unfairly benefiting from state aids.

7 Industry

The European Community has a history of intervening in industrial affairs. The precursor of the EEC, the European Coal and Steel Community was set up for that very purpose. During the 1980s the practice and even use of the term 'industrial policy' fell into disrepute in many western countries, largely as a reaction to the failures of government intervention. During the 1970s following a series of recessions, most European economies were faced with significant industrial restructuring in some major industries: ship-building, textiles, steel manufacture, and cars for example. Government's ability to 'pick winners' or distort markets was shown to be weak.

The scale and speed of industrial restructuring should not be under-estimated. Forty years ago manufacturing industry accounted for 40 per cent of UK GDP, it now accounts for only 20 per cent, and less than a quarter of employment. No sectors are protected from these huge changes. By way of example, over the last twenty years, UK manufacture of machine tools has fallen from 70 per cent to 40 per cent of those sold in this country, fridges from 61 per cent to 53 per cent, washing machines from 82 per cent to 49 per cent, shoes from 69 per cent to 30 per cent, clothing from 79 per cent to 56 per cent, and motor-cycles from 66 per cent to just 4 per cent.[40]

Industrial policy has always been more popular in countries with socialist governments, but does seem to be becoming increasingly fashionable. This is not the place for a discussion on the relative merits of government intervention. However, it is accepted throughout the Community that government should not be completely 'hands-off' but does have a role to play in promoting industry's adaptation to new operating conditions. This ranges from simply providing the minimum legal framework to allow market forces to operate efficiently, through to direct intervention in the markets, nationalization and subsidy, both approaches led by the goal of medium-term sustainable growth.

Such an economic framework requires an environment conducive to new market entrants, the development of new markets, products, and skills. This in turn suggests some kind of role for government in education and training, research and development, stable currencies, transport and communications infrastructures, information and advisory services. Furthermore governments have a function as regulator, and protector of consumers, as well as (normally) being the largest procurer of goods and services in a national economy. In a plural society the degree in which it is involved in these areas remains debatable, and moves towards contracting-out and privatization suggest that the role is growing smaller. Nevertheless governments cannot abrogate their responsibilities at a national level, any more than can the European Commission at a Community level.

The Treaty on European Union provides us with a clear picture of the role of the Community in industrial policy, and prescribes a potentially interventionist position:

Article 130

The Community and the Member States shall ensure that the conditions necessary for the competitiveness of the Community's industry exist.

For that purpose, in accordance with a system of open and competitive markets, their action shall be aimed at:

- speeding up the adjustment of industry to structural changes;
- encouraging an environment favourable to initiative and to the development of undertakings throughout the Community, particularly small and medium-sized undertakings;
- encouraging an environment favourable to cooperation between undertakings;
- fostering better exploitation of the industrial potential of policies of innovation, research and technological development.

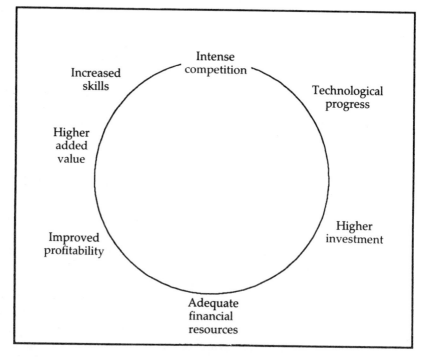

Figure 7.1 *Dynamics of industrial competitiveness*

Of course, the central planks of the Community's industrial policy are completion of the internal market, and the enforcement of a regime for ensuring free and fair competition. Additionally there are policies for transport, energy, employment and education which all impact on industry. Now, however, the European Community has extended its competence into new specific areas for direct action. The target areas are: SMEs, innovation and new technologies, cooperation between undertakings in different member states, and restructuring of targeted industrial sectors, all this without leading to a distortion of competition. Indeed the Commission's stated industrial policy represents the balance of opinion between the economic right free-marketeers, and the political left interventionists, and broadly reflects the sort of consensus within the Commission, the Council of Ministers and the European Parliament. As such it is full of internal contradictions: whilst strengthening optimal allocation of resources by market forces is seen as the key, the existence of an industrial policy acknowledges the scope for intervention to improve industrial competitiveness beyond simply providing the framework of a deregulated level playing field, avoiding making commercial judgements or impinging on the management on enterprises.

The main aim of Community, and indeed other public sector interventions is to 'strengthen the optimal allocation of resources by market forces and towards improving industrial competitiveness and the industrial and particularly technological framework'.[41] This is much more than of academic interest to managers; apart from defining the environment in which commerce and industry must operate, Community industrial policy offers some benefits from its direct intervention, but more importantly some significant signposts as to future trends and strategies to be followed. Companies following strategies of low added-value requiring only minimal investment and skills should be wary of the Commission's judgement that 'The European Community is condemned to technological, commercial and financial, excellence in order to enable the necessary social and environmental expenses to be incurred'. In other words faced with the choice between following the policies and practices of Korea or Switzerland, the EC should only choose the latter.

Competition is the watchword of the industrial policy of the Community, and competitiveness should be the lodestar of European industries. Certain EC industrial sectors have achieved or sustained their own global competitiveness: aerospace, chemicals and pharmaceuticals, for example. There are a number of commonalities between these sectors. First, that they enjoy (or suffer) intense domestic competitiveness, and second they have ensured that they remain at the forefront of technological progress, responding to permanently shortened product life cycles through higher levels of investment in research and development. This in turn generates a requirement for high levels of finance, and therefore profitability, and thus high added-value derived from a penetrating skills base.

Table 7.1 Major EC research programmes

AIM:	Advanced Informatics for Medicine in Europe
BRITE:	Basic Research in Industrial Technologies
BRIDGE:	Biotechnology Research for Innovation, Development and Growth in Europe
DELTA:	Developing European Learning through Technological Advance
DIANE:	Direct Information Access Network for Europe
DIME:	Development of Integrated Monetary Electronics
DRIVE:	Dedicated Road Infrastructure for Vehicle Safety in Europe
ECLAIR:	European Collaborative Linkage of Agriculture and Industry through Research
ESPRIT:	European Strategic Programme of Research and Development in Information Technology
RACE:	Telecommunications
STEP:	Science and Technology for Environmental Protection

A significant aspect to the European Commission's commercial and industrial policy is the recognition of the particular challenges faced by small and medium-sized organizations. As well as a general requirement contained in the Single European Act that legislation should not put an onerous burden on SMEs, the Commission has developed a number of specific initiatives aimed at the improvement of the business environment and the promotion of the development of SMEs in the European Community. Much of this is simply a particular slant to the generality of the single market programme. There are, however specific measures in place to assist SMEs regarding the removal of undue administrative, financial and legal constraints; information and assistance to enterprises; and the encouragement of business cooperation and partnership.

Of note are the measures concerned with public procurement, where the Commission is keen to encourage the practice of staggering payments to SMEs by public sector contractors, which should ease cashflow problems. (It has also decided to improve its own payment practices through the introduction of a standard deadline of 60 days – some would say this is not good enough!)

Of importance is the system for reviewing the impact of EC legislation. Where a proposal is likely to have a significant impact on businesses, the Commission must devise a *fiche d'impacte* statement detailing the potential costs of implementing a proposal. Until January 1991 this only applied to measures put forward to the Council, but has since been extended to all measures. The *fiche d'impacte* deals with the economic consequences on employment, investment and the competitive position of firms within the EC.

On the financial front, the Commission has been examining the particular difficulties faced by SMEs in raising capital. To that end it has set up some twenty-four seed capital funds, operated and coordinated by the European Venture Capital Association, and forty-five projects to promote cross-border pooling of investment in innovative SME projects under the Venture Consort Programme. The Commission is also understood to be examining the potential for mutual guarantee systems, which are very popular in some member states, such as Italy, but virtually unknown in the UK.

The business cooperation network, BC-NET has dealt with more than 58,000 partnership offers or requests since its inception, and has now been extended to all the EFTA countries, as well as Australia, Brazil, Cyprus, Israel, Malta, Mexico, Poland, Argentina, Tunisia and Turkey. BC-NET is essentially an instrument designed to help companies in their search for partners. The Commission notes that when an SME sets out to develop business expansion, whether in the field of commerce, technology or finance, it will tend to use the services of an intermediary, such as a consultant, bank, or chamber of commerce. This is even more likely in the case of transnational cooperation, where SMEs may have to face complex legal and tax problems, as well as language and cultural difficulties.

8 Policies for the regions

The structural upheaval caused by completion of the single market, and economic and monetary union is well in progress, and will clearly result in a positive aggregate performance of the Community as a whole. However, these benefits will not be enjoyed uniformly across the EC, and shifts in regional imbalances will occur.

As has been noted the impetus of economic clustering, speeded up by the removal of barriers to trade is likely to extenuate regional divergence. In particular there is likely to be a heavy concentration of industrial and commercial activity in the 'golden triangle' centred on the Benelux,[42] being at the geographic centre of the Community with excellent transport links to markets, as well as benefiting from a highly trained, flexible and linguistically proficient workforce.

Such a concentration will be at the expense of the peripheral regions of the Community, and there is a real danger that whilst the centre of the EC becomes a highly powered, high added-value, high investment wealth creation zone, the peripheral regions will be reduced to low added-value production (such as screwdriver assembly plants), low skilled and low investment, consumers of wealth, or be confined to agriculture or tourism. Demographic effects would put tremendous strains on public services in such areas, again requiring massive transfer of resources from the richer regions to pay for unemployment benefits, health care and pensions in the peripheral regions.

The Community view on this structural problem is that it is better to address the root causes – the divergence of economic performance, rather than seek to try to treat these symptoms. The Treaty on European Union recognizes this under the opaque title of *economic and social cohesion* with an agreement to reducing the disparities between the levels of development of various regions and the backwardness of the least-favoured regions, including rural areas.[43]

Any regional policy has the inherent commitment to transfer resources from richer regions to poorer regions through a variety of artificial mechanisms. The chosen instruments of the Community are examined below, and each needs to be considered by business for the opportunities or threats to their own competitiveness. This goes beyond decisions as to where to locate premises but should include an assessment of market conditions in different regions, possibilities of market opportunities directly arising in depressed regions, as well as the opportunities for actually carrying out some of the work on behalf of the Commission in implementing its regional policies.

The effectiveness of regional policy has been closely questioned over decades as part of the same debate about regional policy. Providing incentives to companies to move to particular areas to create jobs raises the immediate question as to whether the jobs are additional, or would simply have been created somewhere else. If they are additional, then it is important to consider whether or not the employment is commercially viable without subsidy. With this in mind, projects funded by the Community are decreasingly straight-forward jobs subsidies, and more concerned with facilitating enterprise. On the one hand, new projects such as information and advice centres for new firms and growing SMEs provide appropriate assistance at a local level without distorting commercial decision-making. At the other end of the scale, one aspect of regional policy which does provide a genuine attempt to mitigate some of the disadvantages of poorly performing regions is investment in infrastructure, particularly transport infrastructure. The poorly performing regions of the Community are typified by poor transport networks, poor energy supplies, poor communications systems, as well as a lack of adequate education facilities.

To address these problems of economic and social cohesion, the Community has turned its attention to changes in land use and physical planning. It recognizes that the expected regional migrations of people as well as the ageing of the Community's population will affect urban as well as rural areas. As well as regional policy, other tangential policy areas are:

1 Agricultural policy: generating an efficient agricultural sector, at the same time as encouraging different land use;

Table 8.1   UK regions with below EC average per capita GDP

Northern Ireland
Merseyside
Cornwall, Devon
Clwyd, Dyfed, Gwynedd, Powys
Lincolnshire
Northumberland, Tyne & Wear
Gwent, Mid & SW Glamorgan
Salop, Staffordshire
Hereford, Worcs, Warwick
Lancashire
Dumfries-Galloway, Strathclyde
Derbyshire, Nottinghamshire
Essex
Kent
Highlands & Islands

2 Industrial policy: the need to develop new industrial sites or redevelop old ones;

3 External policy: encouraging inward investment, as well as dealing with migration from non-EC countries, and relations with central and Eastern European countries;

4 Environmental policies: the relationship between the environment and sustainable growth remains key, but this also covers issues relating to quality of life in cities;

5 Human resources policies: the development of new skills in poorly developed regions;

6 Transport policy.

Domestic transport policies of member states have been typified by attempts to relieve congestion in urban areas. The bulk of public expenditure on transport has therefore been devoted to, in particular, road building around major cities. The positive results have been questionable, with significant sections of opinion putting forward the view − with some merit − that increased road building merely generates road demand rather than ameliorating congestion. In any case there is considerable strain between the need to remove congestion, which is a major cost to industry, and environmental protection. It is clear that throughout the Community traffic growth is likely to outstrip improvements to the transport network. From a regional perspective, the imperative is less to relieve congestion in urban areas at the centre of the Community, but to ensure adequate links between regions and major markets.

Relieving the major centres of congestion (the Benelux, the Rhone Valley, Alpine transit routes, and the London−Dover corridor) will undoubtedly be of benefit to industry, but moving commercial transport needs away from these bottlenecks will also contribute to a more even and balanced spread of transport, whilst at the same time stimulating growth in the peripheral regions.

The spread of transport networks is only one aspect of regional transport policy. Changing attitudes and accessibility towards different modes of transport are also important, and should be considered by businesses. In the UK very little freight is moved around on inland waterways, whilst in Germany, for example, canals and rivers contribute a vital part to the transport network. The development of air transport links to the regions is heavily dependent on the economic viability of regional airports − and indeed regional airports have contributed to most of the growth of air transport in the EC. At the same time air congestion − on the ground and in-flight − has increased. Rail transport, currently fashionable on environmental grounds, seems set throughout most of the Community, to enjoy massive investment.

Overall more than 15bn ecus of ERDF spend has been committed to transport infrastructure since 1975. The Commission is committed to increasing spending targeted towards the regions, which should provide incentives and reasons for industry to move back into the peripheral areas. Attention is being given to intermodal transport links, and links between transport networks and other parts of the infrastructure necessary to support thriving industries.

All of commerce and industry has a need for energy. It is forecast that by 1995 there will be no over-capacity in the European Community in the production of electricity. Cheap and efficient sources of electricity and other forms of energy are crucial to the mobility of most industries. The Community is committed to developing new networks for the transmission of energy to ensure an efficient distribution to the peripheral regions. At the same time, there are Community funds available for the development of energy sources suited to the peripheral regions such as wind or tide powered electricity generation.

One of the most efficient means for businesses in the peripheral regions to overcome the structural disadvantages of distance from their markets is the increased use of telecommunications. Telecommunications traffic generates more than 500bn ecus a year around the world, and can only therefore be considered to be a major industry. However, services to less favoured regions remain poor. The aims of the EC are to bring the level of service in the peripheral regions up to the level of the rest of the Community; to introduce new and advanced communications facilities and services in all areas of the EC, including the rural and peripheral regions with ease of access by SMEs and other users in those areas; and to complete any missing links in the networks.

The implications for business of a telecommunications policy for the regions are fairly clear. At one end, the sort of problems businessmen have suffered making calls, and sending faxes from some of the Mediterranean regions should be eased. At the other end, new opportunities for different patterns of work become more efficient and feasible. Remote working, telecommuting, and contracting-out of discrete areas of work, such as data processing to peripheral regions – and thus benefits of lower labour costs – become realistic. Private sector motivations of lower costs and greater efficiencies are clearly in line with the political and social motivations of assisting the regions. As a result of the impact of demographic, social, economic and technical trends, companies are taking a closer look at flexible patterns of work.[44]

One of the manifestations of economic clustering that have been identified is that research and development centres, which do not need to be in close proximity to their marketplaces, have been clustering around public sector institutions such as universities.[45] The establishment of science parks has accelerated this process. The relationship between public and private investment in research and development and regional economic growth is well established.[46] The Commission takes the view that to avoid being disadvantaged a region needs a good level of research and development infrastructure, qualified personnel and a technology transfer capacity. As we have already seen, concentrations, particularly in modern industrial sectors such as electronics and information technology, often cluster around particular locations. Through such projects as the STRIDE initiative, and SPRINT, the Commission is trying to disseminate research findings, and strengthen the infrastructure for innovation.

In the future it seems likely that Community policies in this area are likely to take a greater account of longer-term environmental and resource costs. Sustainable growth will not be achieved at the price of environmental irresponsibility. Environmental protection is probably one of the faster growing commercial sectors in Europe, and we should expect Community intervention in a number of areas. This will provide both new business opportunities, but also considerable restrictions and costs on business activities. Among the environmental challenges faced by the Community are:[47]

- air pollution in industrial conurbations
- supply of water
- soil erosion
- threats to disappearing habitats and species
- pressures on coastal areas
- tourism
- environmental rehabilitation (particularly in eastern Germany)

The central tenets of regional policy are that member states should conduct their internal economic policies in favour of the regions, and the Community itself through the Structural Funds[48] and European Investment Bank. The Regional Development Fund in

Table 8.2 *UK regions with above EC average per capita GDP*

West Yorkshire
Humberside
Dorset, Somerset
Greater Manchester
Borders-Fife-Lothian-Tay
West Midlands
North Yorkshire
Surrey, Sussex
Hampshire & IoW
Leicestershire Northamptonshire
Bedford, Hertfordshire
Avon, Gloucester and Wiltshire
Cheshire
Berks, Bucks & Oxfordshire
Cumbria
Grampian
Greater London

particular is intended to help to redress the main imbalances through participation in the development and structural adjustments of regions whose development is lagging behind and in the conversion of declining industrial sectors. There are, for example, specific schemes for coal-mining regions (RECHAR), steel producing regions (RESIDER) and shipbuilding regions (RENAVAL). Additionally a Committee of Regions, made up of representatives of regional and local authorities, has been established which is consulted where specific regional interests are involved. Further measures include the Integrated Mediterranean Programme (IMP); VALOREN which provides assistance to the development of energy networks to less developed regions, and STAR which is aimed at enabling access to advanced telecommunications in less-favoured regions. The Maastricht Treaty[49] also establishes a new Fund, the Cohesion Fund, which will provide Community financial contributions to projects in the field of environment and trans-European networks in member states with a per capita GDP of less than 90 per cent of the Community average.

Community regional policy has significant impacts for businesses. With the withdrawal of national governments from being providers of state aids, large-scale national regional development programmes are being cut back, but are being replaced at a Community level, by sources of funding for a variety of business activities which may contribute to regional regeneration. The Regional Development Fund Programmes provide to businesses a source of major assistance with new projects. More than 14 billion ecus a year, the equivalent of 3 per cent of EC GDP is currently being dispersed. The availability of such funding is likely to have a significant impact on commercial decision making by businesses examining their locational options.

The current objectives of the funds defined in a June 1988 Council Regulation (2052/88) and Commission guidelines adopted in February 1989 are:

1 Promoting the development and structural adjustment of the regions whose development is lagging behind. This is defined as any region whose GDP is less than 75 per cent of the Community average, in the UK Northern Ireland is the only such designated region. Other regions covered include:

France	—	Départements d'outre-mer, and Corsica
Greece	—	All regions
Ireland	—	All regions
Italy	—	Abruzzi, Basilicata, Calabria, Campania, Molise, Apulia, Sardinia, and Sicily
Portugal	—	All regions
Spain	—	Andalusia, Asturias, Castilla y León, Castilla La Mancha, Ceuta-Melilla, Valencia, Extremadura, Galicia, Canary Islands and Murcia.

2 Converting the regions seriously affected by industrial restructuring. This covers 49 areas in England (none in the South-East, although certain aspects of RENAVAL and RECHAR may apply in Kent), 17 in Scotland, and 14 in Wales.
3 Combating long-term unemployment.
4 Facilitating the occupational integration of young people.
5 Promoting the development of rural areas.

A further secondary objective (of the Social Fund) is the training and professional integration of women, who after a long interruption seek to re-enter the labour market. The types of projects which are eligible for funding under the Structural Funds include measures to stimulate investment which creates jobs, infrastructure projects, measures which help SMEs, collaboration projects between companies, and technology transfer.

Much of this funding is aimed at the public sector, and is used for projects ranging from the completion of the M25 London orbital motorway, to funding of business parks by local authorities. Some business support organizations such as Chambers of Commerce can also benefit from the structural funds. Direct funding available to businesses is more likely to be available through the European Social Fund than the Regional Fund, which is more concerned with job creation and training.

Social Fund support can be used (in the priority regions) for:

- income of trainees (i.e. salaries of employed persons undergoing training)
- wage subsidies
- allowances
- social security and national insurance contributions
- other employer contributions such as bonuses
- daily travelling expenses
- food and lodging for external courses
- salaries for teaching staff, administration and management
- hire and lease of teaching materials or deprecation costs
- advertising of courses
- stationery
- general documentation
- postage and telephone
- water, gas and electricity
- tax and insurance
- child minding

It does not cover bank charges and interest, commissions and payments such as consultancy fees, or rent or lease of property.

Applications for such funds tend to be complex and long-drawn out bureaucratic affairs, which can be off-putting to many businesses.

Nevertheless it should be borne in mind that even if you do not choose to apply for funding that it is available to your competitors.

The Commission will generally match public funds (usually at least 25 per cent of the amount of public expenditure, and not more than 50 per cent of the total cost) for measures which encourage job stability or develop new jobs for the long-term unemployed (aged over twenty-five) in small and medium-sized enterprises (SMEs). It will also cover programmes of vocational training. This is defined by the ESF guidelines as any measure aimed at providing skills necessary to carry out one or more specific types of employment, excluding apprenticeship.

Operation of the funds is complex. Member states (in the UK the Department of Employment) are required to submit to the European Commission outline plans for achieving the objectives of the funds. Part of this is drawn up by the ESF Working Group comprising local authorities, voluntary bodies, ITBs, and the TUC and CBI. The Commission then gives an indication of the financial allocations. Member states are then required to submit operational programmes which contain potential projects in the geographical areas concerned. The Commission in its turn then publishes Community support frameworks, after which details of individual projects, which form part of the operational programmes, are considered by the Department of Employment (typically in November).

In the UK there is a maximum of 200 operational programmes which are structured by organizational type and are compiled at the appropriate national or regional level. Individual projects should be submitted as part of an operational programme. The Department of Employment can advise on this. DE's overall responsibility is for checking basic eligibility and that financial bids are realistic. The Department advises that priority will be given to those projects which encourage job stability and develop new employment opportunities for the long-term unemployed over twenty-five; for those threatened with redundancy as a result of technological modernization in changes in production systems or management structures; and for those employed in SMEs.

Applicants for ESF funding should in the first instance contact the ESF Unit at the Department of Employment, and then the relevant organization responsible for drawing up operational programmes.

EAGGF-Guidance Section has the same objectives 1 & 5 as the ESF and the further objective of speeding up the adjustment of agricultural structures. Like ESF it intervenes horizontally across the Community, but is very closely linked to the Common Agricultural Policy. Considerable business opportunities are likely to arise from the influence of regional policy on agriculture. The future economic development of rural areas will become less dependent on food production, and increasingly concerned with tourism, environmental protection, recreation and forestry.

The Integrated Mediterranean Programme was established after the accession of Spain and Portugal to the Community, and is aimed at Greece, Italy, Southern France and Spain. These are largely agricultural areas, but there are specific measures under the IMP to provide funding for the creation of SMEs, the promotion of tourism, and the establishment of small industrial estates. Further funding is available for vocational training, applied research and the introduction of new technologies.

A specifically politically motivated programme INTERREG also offers benefits to businesses operating in border areas. Around 10 per cent of the Community lives close to a border area, and the Community wishes to encourage cross-frontier activity, as well as to alleviate some of the structural disadvantages from proximity to borders which have in the past inhibited cross-border cooperation, such as being on the end of transport networks, and being artificially separated from natural markets.

For any Community level attempts at influencing regional patterns of growth it is essential that businesses can benefit from a strategic framework provided by local and regional authorities which reflects the longer term pressures and trends identified above. Firms operating in the UK will be at a considerable disadvantage from the lack of a coherent regional structure. Firms operating in the rest of Europe should become acquainted with the local and regional authorities in their areas, their structures and programmes, and their ability to provide assistance.

9 The social dimension and the labour market

There are a number of clear challenges affecting employers in the 1990s, which have been identified and are being addressed by the European Community.[50] Global competition, particularly from the Far East based on high usage of modern technologies on the one hand, and low levels of labour costs on the other are having a considerable impact on competitiveness. If there is not to be a 'fortress Europe' protectionist response to this challenge, then employers themselves will need to respond through improved use of skills and increases in productivity. Cooperation with the countries of Eastern Europe is putting considerable strains on the economies of the West. On the one hand, the pressures of a large new labour resource which has been largely cut off from commercial and technological developments may present a social burden, but it is also an enormous potential for training and development. Technological progress continues rapidly with direct effects on production techniques and communications. In themselves the impact of newer technologies provides an opportunity for different working patterns, but also stimulates the need for rapid adaptation of existing workforces, heightening the need for training and retraining of many segments of the labour market, within organizations themselves, but also as part of the major trend of industrial restructuring.

The intervention of government authorities in the relationship between employers and employees is not a new phenomenon. The UK has had varying degrees of employment protection defined by Acts of Parliament for hundreds of years. An international involvement in national social policies is similarly not new. The UK, along with most other members of the International Labour Organization, has endorsed various conventions in this area. Other international interventions include the European Social Charter of the Council of Europe, and the European Convention on Human Rights. Nevertheless the 'Social Dimension' has proved to be one of the most controversial and political aspects of the development of the EC, which has developed considerably over the past ten years, encroaching significantly on managers' ability and freedom to manage.

In its contribution to the inter-governmental conferences negotiating the Maastricht Treaty the Commission set out the trends it perceived in the social dimension.[51]

1 The internationalization of economies has intensified. The removal

of internal frontiers will lead to substantial transnational integration of firms and increased workforce mobility.

2   Improvement of the competitiveness of firms, by keeping under control and seeking greater flexibility in working conditions and the organization of work, is now a generally recognized imperative. The introduction of new technologies is of major significance here.

3   The quest for competitiveness is being pursued along specifically national lines, but it entails major changes in all member states, with considerable qualitative and quantitative effects on employment and labour relations.

4   The aspirations of workers have altered and diversified. In this way, the needs of firms and the aspirations of individuals have found new areas of convergence is such matters as new forms of employment.

There are broadly four grounds for a European Community dimension on social affairs and employment each of which impinges on commercial activities in the EC:

- **Removal of distortions to competition** – differing degrees of employment protection and working conditions have a considerable impact on unit labour costs, which the Commission would like to see harmonized or approximated as part of its attempts to create a level playing field.
- **Improving the quality of working life** – one of the basic themes of the Community in the 1990s is to create a 'Citizen's Europe' underlining the notion that the EC is not simply an economic community being developed for the benefit of business alone.
- **Stimulating labour mobility** – again a political motivation to encourage a more homogeneous Europe, but also a move towards establishing a more efficient labour market.
- **Encouraging education and training** – one of the most easily identified means of improving global competitiveness.
- **Combating social dumping** – migration of low skilled or unemployed individuals with their families to areas of high social protection would put considerable strains on the economies of particular regions.

The Treaty of Rome includes a specific objective to improve living and working conditions in the Community, as well as various, rather loosely worded articles calling for specific action. These particularly include:

Article 117

Member States agree upon the need to improve working conditions and an improved standard of living for workers so as to make possible their harmonization while the improvement is maintained ...

Article 118

Without prejudice to the other provisions of this Treaty and in conformity with its general objectives, the Commission shall have the task of promoting close cooperation between member states in the social field particularly in matters relating to:

- employment
- labour law and working conditions
- basic and advanced vocational training
- social security
- prevention of occupational accidents and diseases
- occupational hygiene
- the right of associating, and collective bargaining between employers and workers.

To this end the Commission shall act in close contact with member states by making studies, delivering opinions, and arranging consultations at national level and on those of concern to international organizations.

Additionally there are specific Articles, such as Article 119 dealing with equal treatment, and separate provisions dealing with health and safety; freedom of movement and establishment (Articles 48 and 49, 52 to 58), training (Article 128).

Directives raised under the original Treaty of Rome articles include measures dealing with collective redundancies, the transfer of undertakings, insolvency, equal pay, equal treatment, and social security, as well as Health and Safety directives on lead, asbestos, noise, major accidents, which have all been transposed into national legislation in all member states, and form part of the *acquis communautaire*.

The treaty was amended by the Single European Act which strengthened the legal basis for social policy. Most significantly it introduced the concept of qualified majority voting into the Council of Ministers, whereby one country cannot veto a proposal on its own where legislation in connection with completing the internal market is being considered (with exceptions):

Article 100A

1 The Council shall, acting by a qualified majority on a proposal from the Commission, in cooperation with the European Parliament, and the Economic and Social Committee, adopt the measures for the approximation of the provisions laid down by law, regulation or administrative action in member states which have as their object the establishment and functioning of the internal market.
2 Paragraph 1 shall not apply to fiscal provisions, to those relating to the free movement of persons, nor to those relating to the rights and interests of employed persons.

3   The Commission, in its proposals laid down in paragraph 1, concerning health and safety, environmental protection and consumer protection, will take as a base a high level of protection.

Article 118A

1   Member states shall pay particular attention in encouraging improvements, especially in the working environment, as regards the health and safety of workers, and shall set as their objective the harmonization of conditions in this area, while maintaining the improvements made.
2   In order to help achieve the objective laid down in the first paragraph, the Council acting by a qualified majority on a proposal from the Commission, in cooperation with the European Parliament and after consulting the Economic and Social Committee shall adopt by means of directives minimum requirements for gradual implementation, having regard to the conditions and technical rules in member states.

Based on the SEA Articles the Commission put forward its Charter of Fundamental Social Rights, which was signed by all member states except the United Kingdom. This paved the way for the Social Action Programme.

The next step in the development of the social dimension has been the Treaty on European Union which has in the main body of the text, introduced further amendments to the treaty to make the passing of social legislation quicker[52] and to allow for a more

Table 9.1   The Social Action Programme

---

* Organization of working time
* Protection of atypical workers
* Proof of employment
* Individual redundancies
* Protection of young people
* Protection of the elderly
* Transport for disabled employees
* Employee involvement
* Financial participation
* Access to vocational training
* Access to social security schemes
* Protection of pregnant women
* Parental leave and childcare
* Health and safety
* Migrant workers
* Freedom of movement
* Mutual recognition of qualifications
* Equal treatment of men and women

---

interventionist use of the European Social Fund.[53] Most controversially a protocol to the treaty signed by the eleven member states allows proposals raised under the 1989 Social Charter to be agreed without the assent of the United Kingdom. The UK will not be forced to implement such proposals, but the protocol does allow the other eleven to move ahead in this area.

The agreement[54] puts in concrete terms the aims of improved living and working conditions, proper social protection, dialogue between management and labour, the development of human resources with a view to lasting high employment and the combating of exclusion. In particular the agreement allows the Commission to propose directives in the fields of working conditions, information and consultation rights of workers, protection of workers when their contracts are terminated, representation and collective bargaining — including co-determination and equal pay, thus greatly extending the scope for EC intervention in the labour market, and more particularly in the conditions of employment and terms of management for all employees in the EC.

All instruments of social policy have, inherently, a cost attached to them which must be paid by the employer. In certain instances this is a direct financial cost (minimum wages for example), in other cases it is in resulting inflexibility for management or the structures of management. The Department of Employment estimates, for example, that implementing the proposals on part-time and temporary work and parental leave would cost British industry in excess of £4.5 billion a year. Nevertheless there is a genuine desire to improve working and living conditions. This would suggest that the controversy revolves around the price to be paid — and indeed in some instances the value of certain social measures does not seem to be worth the resulting loss of efficiency, or global competitiveness.

There is a fundamental dichotomy of approaches to social policy in the Community, best exemplified by the proposals on part-time work. Within the EC there is a rough match between the number of employers seeking part-time workers, and the number of individuals prepared to work part-time. Changing demographics, the increasing number of women in the labour market and the introduction of new technologies into the workplace, have stimulated the need, and indeed enabled more flexible patterns of work, and there is agreement that this is a constructive approach. However, on the one hand there are those who believe that the best way to stimulate greater use of part-time work is by providing part-time workers with greater employment protection. On the other hand, there is the belief that employers can only be stimulated to provide part-time working by deregulating part-time employment. The two diametrically opposed stances broadly reflect the positions of the European Commission and the United Kingdom Government (and most of its managers). At the heart of debate over the social dimension is the question of whether labour market efficiency is arrived at through increasing employment protection and improving working conditions, or whether deregulation resulting in greater labour market flexibility will make for a more efficient labour market, and a framework for the growth of self-employment, and small firms.

After more than a decade of Conservative government committed to deregulation and the removal of employment protection, UK managers have benefited from a more flexible approach to recruitment, and management of labour. Nevertheless the approaches, and basic aims set out in most of the EC's social proposals represent good management practice and should not be ignored. The detailed impacts of the proposals will be considered in Chapter 16, but it is worth noting at this point some of the issues which will affect businesses in the Community, and the differences in experiences likely to be enjoyed (or suffered) between UK and other EC industries, as well as the likely developments.

The main issues for consideration by EC managers fall into four broad headings:

- Management flexibility
- Compliance costs
- Effects of competitiveness
- Industrial relations

UK managers cannot afford to be complacent about the 'opt-out' from the Maastricht protocol. On the face of it, being exempted from potentially costly legislation should give the UK a considerable competitive advantage over other EC member states, with UK industries benefiting from lower direct labour costs, and an enhanced ability to attract inward investment. There must remain, however, some doubts as to whether the ability to opt-out will actually result in lower *unit* labour costs if productivity improvements are not gained through derogation. Companies which exploit the lower unit labour costs by increasing profit margins, will quickly lose any competitive edge. Furthermore, it is highly questionable how sustainable the UK opt-out is in the longer term. A change of government in the UK would mean the swift introduction of all the Social Charter proposals.

As UK businesses become more internationalized, and operate in different member states, managers in sites overseas will have to conform with the EC social legislation. This will result in the untenable situation of employees of the same company operating in one member state benefiting from high levels of employment protection and working conditions, while employees based in the UK will not. Corporate human resources policies, designed to establish a Europeanized workforce, benefiting from enhanced labour mobility, and capitalizing on the extension of the skills based offered within the single market, will be stretched to the limit to accommodate such divergence. Apart from the difficulties arising simply from offering the same workers different conditions depending on where they are, considerable problems are likely to arise in attracting skilled labour from other member states without offering comparable levels of employment protection and working conditions. A Dutch worker, for example, is highly unlikely to be prepared to forego the generous maternity benefits available under EC law to come to work in the UK. It is not, therefore, in the best interests of UK managers to ignore what is happening in the rest of the EC with regard to social legislation. The derogation from the Social Policy Chapter may provide UK companies with a short-term competitive advantage but it is realistic to suggest that UK companies will have to conform, one way or another, with the policies being established. Demographic changes, and approaches to quality and skills mean that the labour market will itself become a competitive market, with employers competing to attract the best employees. An enlightened management will not succeed, simply providing the minimum working conditions prevalent in the country of operation for its workforce.

Paradoxically the Commission recognizes that in practice, decentralization has been a consistent phenomenon in employee relations across the EC. Over the past ten years wage controls, for example, have been relaxed in the UK, Belgium, Denmark, France, Italy and The Netherlands. A wider range of issues are being moved down from a national, governmental level, to a firm level. Within companies, the practice of employee relations has similarly moved from one based on collective bargaining to one centred around individual negotiation.

The other side of this particular coin relates to the impacts on competitiveness. The Commission has argued at great length, and with some justification, that divergent employment legislation has distorted competition within the Community. Compliance costs, inflexibilities, and direct costs such as pensions and social security, add considerably to the competitive equation. Implementing stringent health and safety laws, for example, can significantly affect productivity. A more lax approach could give a company the edge in European markets. Many of the proposals raised under the Social Charter have as their justification the elimination of such distortions.

Faced with the need to harmonize employment costs it has opted to harmonize employment conditions at the highest level. The Commission has accepted that there are costs involved, but counters that these costs are being suffered equally by all commerce and industry in the EC, so the level playing field is created.

The social dimension has provided one of the most important battlefields for the debates on subsidiarity. Apart from forcing its 'opt-out' the UK government has failed to prevent Community social legislation from becoming more detailed and prescriptive. For UK managers looking towards compliance this may mean adopting increasingly inflexible practices.

As with most Community law, social legislation is being formed through the instruments of treaty requirements, and directives which require transposition into national law. Managers should however, be extremely cautious of direct applicability of treaty requirements where there is no UK law. Most UK employment law – particularly that governing equal treatment – has been introduced following European Court of Justice rulings finding the UK in contravention of its treaty obligations. Recent developments now make it clear that direct applicability can, in certain circumstances, extend beyond governments and the public sector, to private sector organizations.

This notion of each business having an equal handicap is a curious one that has an internal logic but ignores the impacts on competitiveness with the rest of the world. If European Community industry has to bear the cost of high levels of health and safety, generous social security schemes, and inflexible conditions of employment, whilst competitors in the United States, or South-East Asia benefit from cheap labour, deregulation and flexibility, EC companies will find their competitiveness seriously eroded. The Commission's answer to this charge is a simple one: implementing high levels of employment protection and improving working conditions will stimulate employee commitment and increases in per capita productivity greater than the costs of compliance. Management's challenge is to accept that the single European market is not simply, what David Williamson, EC Secretary General, calls a 'cash register' operation, and, possibly against their better judgements to prove the Commission right.

All the above is not simply to suggest that the social dimension is merely a handicap for business to cope with. Opportunities for establishing a framework for the labour market to operate more effectively are arising, particularly in the context of increased labour mobility.

The levelling of the commercial playing field means that the quality of the labour force becomes a more important competitive weapon. Companies unable to benefit from protectionism, or other unfair advantages, will be exposed to demands for competent management, higher quality output, and more efficient productivity. The management of skill shortages will certainly be one of the more difficult challenges facing EC managers over the next twenty years, in the face of changing demography. The opportunities presented by a larger pool of skilled labour are considerable, and should be taken advantage of, along with the benefits of direct Community intervention in education and training, where significant resources are being channelled in the development of Europeanized labour through cultural exchanges, languages programmes and student mobility packages.

Social dumping is the other side to the coin of economic clustering. It refers to the issues of comparative advantage considered in Chapter 1; whilst the clusters are likely to attract highly-skilled labour seeking higher reward from higher added-value industries, there is a danger that low-reward low value-added regions, where there is a reasonably high level of employment and social security protection, will attract the unemployed, and low-skilled. The Social Action Programme is largely an attempt to dampen down the effects of clustering and dumping, nevertheless competitive labour market forces are likely to prevail. These notions are largely theoretical until the market is effectively working, but do present opportunities for companies which do not need to be in close proximity to their markets, and can take advantage of the lower unit labour costs of the poorer performing regions. Regional divergence is considerable, but already it is clear that at a national level labour costs are below the EC average in Greece, Portugal, Spain, Ireland and the United Kingdom.

10 Consumer protection

Bringing down the barriers to trade within the free-trading area of the European economic space is intended to stimulate consumer demand through greater aggregate choice, enhance efficiency, and above all competition. Nevertheless, as has already been noted, the single market has not been devised to be solely of benefit to commerce and industry. It is a homogeneous policy which includes the Citizen's Europe, concern for environmental policy, and improvement of living and working conditions.

The ability for goods and services to be freely traded throughout the Community stemming from the principle of mutual recognition comes with strings attached, most particularly those relating to consumer protection. The precedent setting Cassis de Dijon case laid down that any product legally manufactured and sold in one member state could be sold in another *unless different standards could be justified on health and safety grounds*. There is an expectation that all consumers should be protected from faulty goods and should have redress. So that consumer protection is not used as an excuse to reintroduce national barriers to trade within the Community it is a major area for EC intervention that encompasses safety, but also trading terms, and is a major plank of the level playing field, benefiting competitive and efficiently managed organizations. On the one hand harmonizing levels of consumer protection at the highest levels[55] throughout the Community significantly increases compliance costs, but on the other, it prevents competitors from under-cutting by manufacturing cheaper to produce, but more dangerous goods.

In addition to the competition regulations preventing abuse of market dominance, consumer protection legislation covers a wide range of areas within the relationship between consumer and producer:

- Health and safety
- Faulty goods
- Advertising, labelling and packaging
- Terms of trade, such as consumer credit, implementation of guarantees and after-sales services and door-step selling

This is generally speaking an area of internal market legislation which falls under the heading of increased regulation rather than deregulation. The single largest impact will be that of compliance costs, and quality management. Most EC legislation in this area has already been transposed into national legislation, and the prevailing use of the EC safety symbol is an obvious measure of the encroachment of Community intervention at this level which affects goods manufacturers, service suppliers, distributors and retailers at every level of the supply chain until it reaches the consumer. Distribution policy will be examined in Chapter 18, but the importance of consumer protection law should be examined at an early stage in the development of strategies for bringing goods and services to market. The ability to conform with stringent legislation and regulations will be considerably affected by chosen structures and the management controls of mechanisms such as the use of agents, franchisers, subsidiaries etc.

The most important proposal, implemented in the UK through the Consumer Protection Act is the Product Liability Directive[56] which places strict liability on manufacturers, importers, distributors and retailers for defective goods, irrespective of fault. Significantly consumers no longer have to prove negligence, only fault. Options for redress are considerable and go beyond replacement of faulty goods or refunds, but also cover liability for secondary damage. In theory if a toaster is defective and sets fire to a house then the manufacturer, distributor or retailer is liable for the cost of damage to the house, as well as to the toaster. The implications for efficient quality control mechanisms throughout the distribution chain are therefore considerable.

Table 10.1   Consumer protection directives

- Product liability
- Textile names
- Sale of saccharin
- Fire safety of hotels
- Goods appearing as others
- Prepackaged liquids
- Measuring containers
- Measurement of weight or volume
- Labelling, presentation and packaging of foodstuffs
- Labelling of energy consumption
- Pricing of foodstuffs
- Misleading advertising
- Consumer contracts negotiated away from business premises
- Consumer credit
- Indication of alcoholic content
- Foodstuffs
- Pharmaceuticals
- Chemical products
- Construction products
- Toys

The misleading and unfair advertising directive[57] along with specific directives on the advertising of alcohol and tobacco strictly regulate marketing of products in the Community. Of increasing relevance in this area are regulations covering broadcasting and advertising to children. Also of interest is the directive allowing comparative advertising which until recently was only permitted in the UK and The Netherlands. Companies examining marketing strategies will need to conform closely with EC regulations, particularly if they are planning cross-border advertising campaigns.

Door-to-door selling is regulated under the directive governing the negotiation of contacts away from business premises, which introduced cooling-off periods. Exclusion include products worth less than 100 ecus (e.g. brushes), and milk.

The directive on consumer credit is a major part of the Commission's policy on making consumer transactions more transparent and educating the consumer. The existing requirement to display the annual percentage rate (APR) in consumer credit contracts is a conformance with this directive.

Other legislation which has already been implemented throughout the Community which stems from EC consumer protection law are the sell-by and eat-by dates on foodstuffs, and laws preventing the sale of goods which look like food but are not. (This does not apply to goods such as ornamental fruit, but aims to protect, in particular children, from such items as erasers in the shape of confectionery.)

Responsibility for compliance with consumer protection legislation should not simply fall with production managers, but also within the marketing responsibility. Strict controls on labelling, and packaging apply, such as the need to price foodstuffs in a way which allows comparison – showing the price per kilogramme for example. The directives on price indication require all goods which are sold in bulk to have the price clearly displayed.

Data protection legislation, largely conceived to protect the privacy of the individual has been extended to consumer protection, with proposals (so far unadopted) to prohibit the use of computers to make assumptions about an individual's spending intentions. The second data protection directive would, if adopted, prevent a company selling, for example, mobile telephones, from using a computer to generate a list of people who have bought high-performance cars and are therefore likely to buy their product.

In the same manner as environmental standards set by national authorities endanger the establishment of the internal market, consumer protection policy which sets minimum levels of protection throughout the Community, but which allows member states to implement higher standards also presents problems to businesses seeking to develop products and services which may freely be marketed throughout the Community. There is a real threat to the Cassis de Dijon ruling as a basis for the internal market through progressive and incremental policies aimed at protecting European

Consumer protection **83**

Table 10.2   Consumer protection in the Treaty on European Union

Article 129a

1   The Community shall contribute to the attainment of a high level of
consumer protection through:
   (a)   measures adopted pursuant to Article 100a in the context of
      completion of the internal market;
   (b)   specific action which supports and supplements the policy pursued by
      the member states to protect the health, safety and economic
      interests of consumers and to provide adequate information to
      consumers.
2   The Council, acting in accordance with the procedure referred to in
Article 189b [qualified majority adoption] and after consulting the Economic
and Social Committee, shall adopt the specific action referred to in
paragraph 1(b).
3   Action pursuant to paragraph 2 shall not prevent any member state from
maintaining more stringent protective measures. Such measures shall be
compatible with this treaty. The Commission shall be notified of them.

consumers. The Maastricht Treaty opens up a considerable loophole
which may lead to the re-establishment of national non-tariff barriers.
This type of policy has yet to be tested in the courts, but is likely to
present considerable problems for exports and importers in the
future. The capacity to introduce more stringent regulations seems
to conflict directly with the free movement of goods. In the meantime,
firms should not solely rely on conforming with EC legislation on
consumer protection, but will also have to research and conform
with any additional national or local regulations.

11 Public procurement

Purchasing by the public sector accounts for more than 15 per cent of the European Community's GDP. It therefore constitutes an important part of the internal market, where the principle that goods should move freely applies equally. And yet, whereas private sector import penetration averages above 20 per cent in the Community, the award of public sector contracts to foreign companies remains less than 5 per cent, even though in some sectors, such as railways, telecommunications and energy the public sector accounts for up to 90 per cent of all purchases. Since 1970 the EC has been trying to eradicate discriminatory practices in the award of public sector contracts through a series of measures:

- Supply of goods directive EEC/70/32
- Award procedures for public works directive EEC/71/305 & EEC/89/440
- Freedom to provide services EEC/71/304
- Public supply contracts EEC/77/62 & EEC/80/767 & EEC/88/295
- Building works EEC/89/440
- Utilities EEC/90/531

Nevertheless procurement practices by central and local government and its agencies, such as defence, police, health and education authorities have continued to be biased against foreign suppliers. This has had a considerably inhibiting effect on the development of the internal market and presents a challenge to the private sector. National policies which discriminate in favour of local suppliers have succeeded in ensuring market fragmentation, inefficiency and waste, in protecting a number of industries in their home markets without successfully providing value for money for public services. Companies currently depending on public contracts will increasingly find themselves open to greater competition.

The aim of the EC's public purchasing policies and regulations are explicit: to open up these markets and actively encourage foreign companies to tender for public contracts, particularly smaller companies who historically have not bid, or have been unsuccessful bidders for public contracts. (The Commission was understood to have even considered requiring a percentage of large public sector contracts to be awarded to or sub-contracted to SMEs.)

Any public sector (which includes private sector companies which are regulated or largely influenced by the public sector, such as water companies, British Telecom, or work contracted *to* the private sector by the public sector) contract above 200,000 ecus for local government, and 134,000[58] ecus for central government must conform with the procedures laid down in the above directives. This requires that they be published in the *Official Journal of the European Communities*, and there can be no discrimination between bidders on the grounds of nationality.

There are broadly three types of contract procedures: open, restricted or negotiated. In the open procedures any company in the Community has the right to bid and at least fifty-two days notice must be given. A restricted procedure allows the buyer to limit the amount of bidders – but not on grounds of nationality, by inviting bids. At least forty days notice must be given. The negotiated procedure is only allowed in certain circumstances, principally the exclusions for security or cultural grounds, or where there is an urgent need for supply.

Tenders must be awarded to the lowest priced, or most effective bidder; 'the most economically advantageous' irrespective of where the company is based.

It is important to note that public contractors may be required to conform with the quality management standard EN29000 (BS5750). Suppliers may need to provide evidence of their ability to deliver, and contractors may define certain criteria in advance as well as technical standards which need to be met. These must be published in advance, and are not allowed to be directly or indirectly discriminatory. It would, for example, be contrary to the directives for a local council to insist that a contract was performed (or created jobs) by a local labour force.

Contracts for civil engineering and construction works need to be for more than 5 million ecus. Invitations to tender must be published in the *Official Journal*, and are also accessible electronically though the Tenders Electronic Daily (TED).

Table 11.1   Public procurement

Country	Public spend
Belgium	£15.3bn
Denmark	£17.4bn
France	£77.4bn
Germany	£98.2bn
Greece	£8.1bn
Netherlands	£22.3bn
Ireland	£3.5bn
Italy	£104.3bn
Luxembourg	£0.7bn
Portugal	£4.5bn
Spain	£38.1bn

Until recently the public procurement directives did not cover energy, water, transport and communications – the so-called 'excluded sectors'. This gap has now been filled, with the only exemptions remaining being for oil, gas and coal exploration, and also certain conditions relating to security or cultural causes.

The Commission has significant powers to invoke infringement procedures where a company feels that it has been discriminated against. The implications for the private sector are considerable bearing in mind the size of the marketplace, as the thresholds are relatively low. Tendering for public sector contracts throughout the Community is certainly not just the preserve of large companies, or indeed large contracts.

For managers in the public sector the public procurement policies represent increased regulation, but also policies which should lead to greater competition and efficiency. For managers in the private sector, the opening up of public contracts presents a considerable market opportunity (and threat to the complacent). Already the streets of Brighton are being cleaned by a Spanish company. Companies should make the most of any comparative advantage they have to seek out and win public sector contracts. UK companies, for example, benefit considerably over most other EC companies from having relatively low unit labour costs, or employment overheads. Employing people in the UK to work on contracts in another member state may give sufficient competitive edge.

It should be noted that the public procurement policy has been extended to cover the service sector, which provides the largest opportunity for participation by SMEs. All public contracts likely to be worth more than 140,000 ecus, in such areas as maintenance, courier services, printing, building cleaning and advertising would be subject to the regime of publishing tenders in the *Official Journal* and non-discrimination.

To put this area of policy into perspective, the central and local government bodies in the United Kingdom spend more than £25 billion a year.[59] Her Majesty's Stationery Office buys more than £400 million of print, stationery and office supplies. The Post Office spends in excess of £380 million a year. The opportunities throughout the EC are therefore considerable, and require attention by all private sector sellers. Whilst the perception may remain that public authorities continue to discriminate against foreign bidders and thus it is not worth the trouble or expense against bidding, this is largely an untested perception as the numbers of foreign bidders remain extremely small.

12 European networks

Completion of the Single Market, development of the European Economic Area, and the overall levels of economic growth which result, as well as the expansion of the service sector, and the increased use of such management methods as just-in-time will put unprecedented demands on the European transport, communications and energy networks. The volume of transport has been growing by nearly 5 per cent a year, faster than the economy as a whole.[60] More than 1,000 billion tons of freight move across the transport network. The Community has taken upon itself two roles with regard to the development of trans-European networks. First their development, and second a more efficient working of the existing transport market – or what the Commission calls spatial coherence.

Of all the areas of the internal market which affect commerce and industry none are probably so immediately relevant to the development of trade, but this is the area where there has been the least

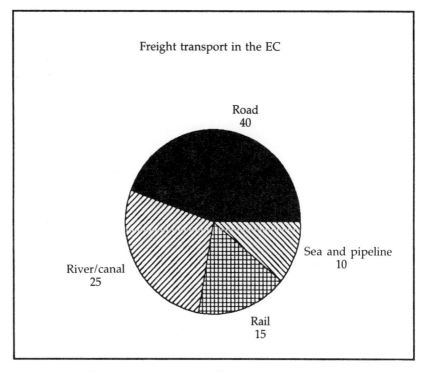

Figure 12.1 *Freight transport in the EC*

progress. Indeed in 1985 the Court of Justice delivered a reprimand to the Council of Ministers for their failure to take the necessary decisions to develop a European transport policy. A casual observer looking at air fares between major EC cities will easily see that the benefits of a free market are not yet apparent, so long as it is cheaper to fly from London to New York, than from London to Brussels. There is, nevertheless, a major programme of liberalization in progress which will have significant benefits to businesses working in Europe, translated into more efficient and cheaper transport of goods and passengers; diminishing the economic distances between producers and their markets.

Road transport has historically been heavily regulated and dominated by cartels. The fifty or so EC regulations on road transport (covering such issues as common driving licences, tachometers, speed limits, axle weights etc.) are important in opening up the market, but beyond the scope of this book. Of major importance will be the changes to cabotage. This is the practice of foreign hauliers picking up and delivering goods in another member state, often on their way through. Lorries travelling from Edinburgh to Rome, fully laden on the way out, have, in the past been prevented from picking up goods on their way back, thus, in effect, doubling the economic cost of intra-Community transit. Enablement of cabotage in road haulage will dramatically reduce costs, both directly, as well as by introducing greater levels of competition at the centre of the network. Haulage within the UK and other peripheral regions is unlikely to benefit, but exporters as well as importers should enjoy a reduction in their transport costs.

The field of air transport has proved to be almost intractable. Stuffed with subsidies, and national quotas, tariffs, limits on capacity, rigid methods of slot allocation, more than 200 bilateral agreements and traffic control congestion, little visible progress has been made. Air transport is of immediate importance to the business traveller, particularly from the UK and Ireland — and therefore for the development of new business opportunities, but of increasing importance to the high-value-added industries where rapid delivery of mail and cargo is vital. Community level intervention on fares, routes and flow management is slowly progressing, but it will be many years before there is true liberalization of the airways in Europe.

Liberalization of European transport, under the heading of removal of physical barriers to trade should reduce costs by between a third and a half. Cecchini uses the example of two 1,200 km trips — one within the United Kingdom, and one from London to Milan. The first took thirty-six hours, the second (excluding time taken actually to cross the Channel) took fifty-eight hours because of delays at borders. The increasing efficiency of the transport network coupled with the removal of physical barriers should be a major factor in managing the single market. At the same time, however, the conflicting lines of thought on preserving the environment should be considered. The introduction of carbon taxes will mitigate against long-distance travel by road, and in favour of rail, along with the suggestions of making heavy-goods vehicles pay more for use of the networks.

Transport policy of the 1980s was greatly centred around reducing congestion in the urban areas in the centre of Europe, rather than improving the infrastructure in the peripheral regions. The themes of transport development in the 1990s will be more towards developing the infrastructure in the peripheral regions. Of course, pressures will intensify around the major industrial areas, the populous conurbations and the trunks which link the Rhine–Ruhr valleys, Greater London, the Randstad, Ile de France, Munich and Milan – the golden banana, and it is likely that capacity will not meet demand. Environmental pressures will prevent the provision of new capacity. The room for growth therefore lies where there is spare capacity – inland waterways and rail. In the United Kingdom both modes have fallen off in industrial popularity suffering from reputations for inefficiency, unreliability and lack of economy. However, the more progressive development of inter-modal transport coupled with much higher levels of public subsidy has permitted a continental system of rail and canal which is the envy of the rest of the world.

Congestion of the road is likely to lead to traffic management systems being introduced throughout Europe, whether at a local level or Europe-wide. Road charging schemes, tolls on urban motorways or artificial methods of managing demand, such as taxes on particular road users, are all under consideration and need to be borne in mind when considering the transport implications of a single market.

The creation of a more balanced transport network across the EC is a stated priority:

> Within the framework of a system of open and competitive markets, action by the Community shall aim at promoting the interconnection and inter-operability of national networks as well as access to such networks. It shall take account in particular of the need to link island, landlocked and peripheral regions with the central regions of the Community.[61]

A major political obstacle needs to be overcome if the desire to promote economic development in the regions is to be satisfied through fulfilling the transport requirements of business. In economies, such as the UK, where the free-market approach is in the ascendancy, transport investment tends to follow private sector industrial development, because it is more difficult to identify and quantify the return on investment. Narrow cost-benefit analysis usually fails to stimulate infrastructure investment. In other words, only once a demand has been created, will the public sector seek to satisfy it through new roads. Such an approach can clearly be

Table 12.1 Planned transport developments

Road:
- Toulouse → Madrid
- Bordeaux → Valencia
- Crewe → Holyhead
- Patra → Athens

Rail:
- Paris → London → Brussels → Amsterdam → Cologne
- Seville → Madrid → Barcelona → Lyon → Turin → Milan → Venice

---

seen in the problems suffered at such developments as Canary Wharf in London, and Trafford Park in Manchester. In more planned economies, state investment in the infrastructure precedes, and stimulates private sector investment.

The lack of an efficient high-speed rail network in the UK should not blind British managers to the potentials of rail on the continent. 80 per cent of the continental railway system is run at more than 70 km an hour. The main urban links run at an average of 120 km an hour. Considerable attention is being given to ensuring that whilst the urban rail network becomes more efficient, good connections between rural areas, airports, and seaports are also being established.

One of the more significant competitive weapons at the disposal of businesses is access to and management of information. The past decade has seen the mushrooming of information technology in business. Just ten years ago companies using personal computers and facsimile machines were the exception, now they are the rule. The spread of information technology and telecommunications (ITT) has had a considerable impact on the way in which companies are structured, can be managed, and interface with the market. Telecommunications traffic is expected to expand at between 15 per cent to 20 per cent a year for the next ten years[62] and with it opportunities for improving productivity, distribution and marketing, as well as increasing flexibility, speed and responsiveness to customer needs.

The effective use of ITT has the potential to reduce the comparative disadvantages of distance to nothing, enabling a greater dispersal of operations. At one end of the scale, ITT permits changes to the organization of work − telecommuting etc., whilst at the other end, whole sections of corporate activities can be performed remotely where labour costs are lower. British Telecom, for example, now operates most of its directory enquiry services in the UK from Scotland with operators working from home. Several companies have moved their data processing functions across the world. Managers can now afford to consider the actual needs of location without the hindrance of distance.

The impacts on organizational structures, and human motivation need to be addressed. Nevertheless, the trend is for small concentrations of 'head office' activities, with a decentralization of peripheral services – often to peripheral regions. Many consumer services can now be delivered to a greater local density through ITT – telebanking, teleshopping, video conferencing, travel arrangements, inventory management, education and training, sales support etc. The spread of ITT throughout the Community is progressing at an uneven pace. The United Kingdom enjoys the highest density of personal computers, but lags behind France in its use of telecommunications. Other countries such as Italy and Holland are rapidly developing Videotex services. At the opposite end of development, parts of the Mediterranean, and most of Eastern Europe still suffer from a very poor quality of even basic telecommunications infrastructure. The European Commission estimates that the poorer performing regions (those qualifying for Objective 1 ERDF support) are roughly ten years behind the more advanced regions.

Recognizing the importance of telecommunications networks in promoting an efficient economic framework, the European Commission has developed a number of schemes to promote its development including STAR, TELEMATIQUE and PRISMA.

Commerce and industry, particularly the manufacturing sector are heavily dependent on a secure supply of gas and electricity at competitive prices. The development of integrated transmission networks as well as new energy generation capacity, will, like the development of new telecommunications and transport networks, greatly enhance the ability of companies to maximize the opportunities of trading in the single market, opening up new possible territories within the EC which have hitherto been unable to support a viable manufacturing industry.

Against the background of no growth in nuclear electricity generation, environmental pressures against the burning of coal, and declining production of oil, competition for energy will become intense. Already there are wide disparities in pricing, which often result from cross-subsidies between the industrial and domestic consumers. Industrial electricity prices in Ireland and the UK are at around 85 per cent of the EC average, whilst Danish manufacturers suffer from prices which are about 60 per cent above the EC average. As yet there are no proposals to harmonize electricity prices, although certain aspects of state subsidization of energy costs are being examined under competition policy. The thrust of Community energy policy is towards greater efficiency in generation and consumption of energy, as well as more flexible cross-border transmission networks, which should stimulate greater competition and therefore lower costs. Completion of the internal energy market will be of considerable benefit to all businesses. As well as expanding the availability of energy and access to new regions, the ability of business to shop around for its energy supplies across frontiers will greatly enhance efficiency and cost-competitiveness.

13 Environmental policies

Environmental concerns have, to date had a relatively minor impact on the European Community, and may have been largely ignored by managers. However, the Treaty on European Union introduces a framework for 'a policy in the sphere of the environment' requiring 'a harmonious and balanced development of economic activities, sustainable and non-inflationary growth respecting the environment'.[63] Managers need to be mindful of the implications of existing and potential EC environmental legislation, particularly on their costs throughout the operation, as well as the wider social implications of greater public awareness and discrimination regarding environmental responsibility.

The EC has had four environmental action programmes and is now implementing the fifth which involves a heightened Community involvement. The environment is used as an umbrella heading for a number of issues which have direct effect on EC businesses going far beyond more straightforward issues such as pollution control.

Virtually all organizations are affected by environmental considerations, whether they pollute, use energy, or generate waste. Manufacturing industry is therefore selected as one of the five targets of the action programme. As a management discipline the environment is a relatively new one, where expertise is in short supply, the issues complex, and the threats and opportunities considerable. In the main, the Community is attempting to pursue the line that sustainable economic growth will not be possible without environ-

Table 13.1 Environmental management

Air quality management
Waste resource management
Soil quality maintenance
Conservation
Energy
Demography
Packaging
Waste management
Pollution controls
Physical planning
Infrastructure planning
Traffic management
Risk and accident management

mental responsibility. Others argue that the reverse is equally true, and there is considerable tension between these at times conflicting points of view, with industry often caught in the cross-fire. However, a positive perspective on the environmental question is that increasing demand for new clean technologies will stimulate new market opportunities and considerable savings can be enjoyed by industry from energy and resource efficiency.

The Commission recognizes that this is a highly complex issue which cannot simply be resolved by a directive requiring commerce and industry to 'act in a sustainable manner'. The number of instruments being used to enforce EC policy on managers range from the persuasive (grants, information schemes etc.) to the controlling (emissions limits) and include such voluntary mechanisms as eco-labelling, as well as mandatory harmonization measures such as minimum packaging standards. Other instruments include structural planning, environmental audits, tradeable emission permits, integrated pollution control mechanisms, and inventories of discharges and waste and fiscal measures such as carbon taxes.

Even though manufacturing industry has been selected as a particular target, managers in other sectors cannot afford to be complacent as to the implications on their own organizations. Apart from consumer pressures, they will be indirectly affected by the impact on the targets, in particular those relating to the transport and energy sectors. (Organizations involved in tourism need to be especially mindful). Unlike the United Nations, the European Community is a legislative body, and has every intention of using its powers to influence management behaviour.

The starting point for the Community, and therefore businesses, is to acquire a better and more reliable understanding of the issues, and an accurate observation of the current situation. This is a particularly opaque area, where major themes such as the theory of global warming remain the subject of intense scientific debate and controversy. Collection of information is therefore a priority and one which may impact on business in a number of different ways, the most striking of which is probably the development around the EC of registers of contaminated land, which will include land which is potentially contaminated. Access to such information will have a dramatic effect on such things as land prices, stimulating, it is hoped, clean-up. Clean-up costs of contaminated land are variously estimated as being between £100,000 and £1m an acre. With nearly a third of the West Midlands being potentially contaminated, the prospects for business costs are quite awesome. Ignorance may currently be bliss, but knowledge of potential liabilities is likely to be forced on managers, and with knowledge will come the cost. Immediate and urgent action is therefore to implement eco-auditing programmes.

One significant change in the Fifth Action Programme from its predecessors is the recognition that environmental responsibility has a value and therefore a market approach to the environment may be an effective one. The environment therefore becomes a bottom line consideration, from energy costs through to waste penalties. As a starting point the Commission is suggesting that companies should disclose in their annual reports details of their environmental expenses, and make financial provision for future environmental liabilities.

It is clear that left to its own devices a competitive market driven by the profit motive is unlikely to put a high value on environmental responsibility. Mismanagement of natural resources, environmental accidents, and excessive pollution are the legacy of the free market which is inherently short-term in its outlook. The Community is seeking to intervene directly in the market to ensure that a high value is placed on environmentally friendly behaviour throughout a product life-cycle: cradle to grave sourcing, production, distribution, consumption, and disposal. On the one hand this is an internal market question: economic operators who are environmentally friendly should not be competitively disadvantaged against other operators who are not incurring the costs of responsible use of resources, effective waste management etc. On the other hand, by raising environmental standards and therefore costs on industry throughout the Community there is a real danger of damaging the competitiveness of EC commerce and industry in global markets.

The principle that lies behind adding value to environmental responsibility is that the polluter should pay. This notion first emerged from the OECD, and was adopted as a non-binding Recommendation by the EC in 1975. It now forms the foundation for a considerable number of legally binding directives. This manifests itself in systems of charging companies who pollute: fees and levies for factories with outflows into rivers for example. Similarly fiscal incentives can be used to influence behaviour. Taxing the polluter, or providing tax reliefs for the responsible operator introducing newer cleaner technologies are both effective means of changing behaviour. This is most obviously practised by member states who impose a lower excise duty on unleaded petrol. A wide ranging carbon tax (which would add about $10 to the price of a barrel of oil) is envisaged, to stimulate companies to seek alternative sources of energy. Environmental auditing and eco-labelling are both instruments designed to stimulate consumer pressure on economic operators, again by implying a direct value for environmental responsibility.

There are hundreds of environmentally related directives, regulations and recommendations, and a further 2,000 production chemicals are currently being assessed. The principal instruments adopted so far however include:

- **Major accidents (the 'Seveso' directive)**
- **Emissions of sulphur dioxide, dust and nitrogen**

Sets limits for the emissions from large combustion and incineration processes
- **Quality standards for water**
- **Environmental impact assessments for major projects**
  Planning applications for major developments are required to be accompanied by an environmental statement along with details of any representations made by the public before planning permission can be granted.

Directives currently in the pipeline include:

- **Civil liability for waste damage**
  Imposing on both producers and importers a no-fault civil liability for any damage caused by waste. Importers and producers will need to cover themselves with appropriate insurance.
- **Packaging**
  The aim of the Directive is to increase the amount of recycled packaging to 60 per cent. Packaging companies will need to provide detailed information on their processes. Strict limits will be imposed on the amount of metal and other dangerous substances which can be allowed in packaging.
- **Pollution taxes**

An important aspect to the developing code of environmental legislation is the potential for reintroducing non-tariff barriers. Domestic legislation in several member states is outstripping the ability of the Community to agree EC-wide environmental standards. In Germany, for example, stringent packaging, recycling and waste management regulations are already in place, which, *inter alia*, oblige all economic operators to make arrangements for the return by consumers of all packaging. Proposals are also being put forward that all new cars sold in Germany should be 100 per cent recyclable. The Commission can challenge national legislation which it perceives to be a distortion to trade − such as Denmark's attempt to ban metal drinks cans − but cannot act where there is no Community code. The EC has now proposed a packaging directive, but at the time of writing this remains in draft.

The response of business managers to this fast developing area must be two-pronged, both commercial and compliant. Avoiding liability for punitive charges may initially mean a not inconsiderable investment in new cleaner sourcing, production and distribution technologies, but cannot be deferred for long. This has considerable implications for research and development budgets. The commitment of the EC and member states to sustainable development can no longer be questioned. At the same time the responses of consumers are less ambivalent, and there is real evidence that consumers are prepared to pay more for environmentally responsibly produced goods and will be looking for evidence, such as an EC eco-label on goods.

Table 13.2   Industry target activities for environmental protection

- Operating licences
- Emission inventories
- Environmental audits
- Environmental charges
- Clean technologies
- Waste inventories
- Fiscal incentives
- Deposit/return systems
- Civil liability
- Eco-labelling
- Product standards
- Consumer information

The burden of compliance will be very different for different organizations depending on the exact products, substances and processes currently in use, and managers will need to take professional advice on compliance with existing requirements. It is equally important to look ahead to new regulations in the pipeline and other likely developments. Product cycles and lead times, even though they are getting shorter, can still be outrun by the pace of legislative change. All managers need to anticipate and prepare for the changing regulatory framework which may, at a stroke, make a particular process or product illegal or commercial unviable.

Community environmental action for the next ten years, under the Fifth Action Programme will be aimed at meeting a large number of specific targets. All of these will be implemented through the whole range of instruments and need to be carefully considered if they impact, directly or indirectly, on products or processes currently being used. The main targets are:

- Reducing emissions of nitrous oxide by 30 per cent by 2000
- Reducing emissions of sulphur dioxide by 35 per cent by 2000
- Reducing emissions of dioxins by 90 per cent by 2005
- Reducing emissions of cadmium, and lead by 70 per cent by 1995
- Phasing out of noise pollution in excess of 65 dB(A) and banning of public noise levels in excess of 85 dB(A)
- Stabilization of current levels of waste generation.

Two broad approaches are becoming prevalent as a response to managing the European environmental framework. Eco-auditing has made considerable inroads in The Netherlands and Germany, and has also been demonstrated to lead to improvements in general management practices and efficiency savings. This is generally something that can also be done using external professionals who can provide an analysis of land use, raw materials processing, hygiene, and distributive effects, as well as providing recommendations for alternative raw materials, how to avoid and substitute dangerous substances, and other organizational issues. At the same time as the development of eco-auditing, the British Standards Institution has developed a British Standard for environmental management, BS7570, which is akin to the quality management standard BS5750. Eco-labelling remains a voluntary code, and there are no restrictions, beyond the standard requirements for advertisers of truth and honesty, making environmental claims.

The EC eco-label, however, is likely to become the predominant indicator of environmental friendliness. There are, however, already concerns that the details will take too long to work out. It sets a demanding standard of environmental responsibility from the cradle to the grave for individual products. To take washing machines as an example which have a life-span of around thirty years, apart from the more obvious considerations of water pollution resulting from their use, to qualify for an eco-label a washing machine would also have to be demonstrably recyclable, energy economic, efficiently packaged, and responsibly distributed. All the production process from raw materials through to finished goods would also have to be demonstrably environmentally responsible. A separate regulation limits the labelling of products as being energy efficient to those which meet high technical standards.

Very much in the same way that the '1992' issue was largely ignored for many years, and then the initial responses from the corporate sector were weak – such as nominating a single manager to be responsible for Europe – the approach to managing the European environment question has to be an integral part of corporate planning, which affects most functions of any organization.

14 Corporate management

Managers who are running their own businesses, departmental heads in larger organizations, chief executives of small and medium-sized companies, or top men in top companies are all to a greater or lesser extent responsible for putting in place the appropriate frameworks for managing the resources of the organization – time, physical, financial and human resources. Before getting down to the business of conceiving strategies for dealing with the single market, devising tactics, and implementing operations, all managers will need to consider carefully the structures of their organization. To some extent they are confined by the strictures of company law and this section will deal with compliance with the raft of EC company law directives, as well as providing the raw material for efficient strategic structures to meet the challenges ahead.

Much theoretical work has been developed about the structures of organizations, which warrant some attention.[64] In practice no organization is quite the same as another, so while there may be lessons to be learnt, there is no blueprint. Nevertheless a number of common themes have emerged in practice. This is most succinctly described in a BIM report *The Responsive Organization*:[65]

> Organizations are becoming more flexible and adaptable in the face of multiple challenges. Facilitating networks are replacing bureaucracy, procedures are giving way to processes. Delegation and decentralization of roles and responsibilities to line managers is occurring and is likely to continue.

As we have already seen, management of the single European market is inherently the management of change, with a number of major influences at work.

This is not simply a question of devising the appropriate structure to cope with the challenges, opportunities and threats identified so far, but establishing a system of management which stimulates, governs, and engineers responses to continual change. Responsibilities of individuals, and organizational units whether organized horizontally by function, vertically by product, or geographically, are likely to be in a state of continual flux.

The processes of decentralization, delegated responsibilities, subcontracting, modular systems, specialization of professionals, use of project teams, quality assurance, all working in an environment which reflects the turbulence of technological, social, legal and political transformation do not make for a secure foundation based on traditional methods of line-management responsibilities fed down a hierarchical pyramid. Major organizational restructuring is a common fact of life which is an on-going process of adaptation, and should not be perceived as a one-off response to a particular change. Incremental adaptation, or major evolutionary leaps are the major challenges facing managers in Europe in the 1990s with the most direct impacts being felt at the human level. It should never be forgotten that any organization is simply an agglomeration of individuals, who, for the most part, are there by choice. Ensuring that their aspirations match the changing needs of the organization will be crucial. The scope for individuals to define their own areas of operation − to be involved in the management of the company has to increase, and at the same time decision-making is being brought closer to the customer.

We have already seen that the motif of the single market is the strains between centralization and dispersion − between clusters and peripheries, between small and large, between specialized niche markets and pan-Europeanism, and through trans-European networks. To meet these trends, organizational structures need not only to be fluid and flexible, responsive and adaptable, temporary and kinetic, but also to exploit the advantages offered by information technology, meet the ambitions of stakeholders such as employees,

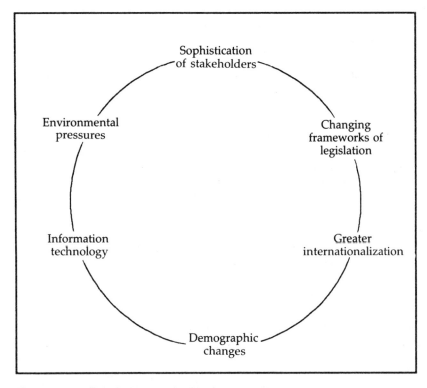

Figure 14.1 *Trends in organizational structures*

customers, sub-contractors, shareholders and the wider community. It is unlikely that traditional pyramidal structures will be appropriate. Flatter structures may be more appropriate as a response, and there has been a clear trend towards removing tranches of middle-managers. But other arrays such as dynamic networks, and matrices which bridge horizontal and vertical remits, functions and ranks, should be considered. At an individual level this will inevitably mean the development on the one hand of the general manager – a multi-functional individual with particular skills in coordination, and project management and the specialist professional.

With hierarchies rapidly disappearing, and the relative ability of all people within or linked to an organization to add value better understood, more flexible structures come into place. The capacity of information technology to allow information (and therefore power and influence) to run both up and down structures of management as well as across networks considerably allows the reduction of bureaucracies which tend to control and command, instead of ser-vicing and enabling. This is a direct consequence of devolution and decentralization. To take the personnel function as an example, most of its purposes – recruitment, motivation, education and development, discipline – should be fulfilled by line managers and not by bureaucrats. Specialist areas such as pay and reward are areas which can be brought in as and where necessary. Very close attention needs to be given to which functions and specialisms need to be retained in-house, and which are more effectively contracted-out.

There is no blueprint for organizational structures. However, taking into account the emerging influences, managers will need to be able to conceive and implement appropriate frameworks to deal with expansion into new territories, dispersal or organization, a reliance on others through sub-contracting, along with the competitive labour market and impacts of new technologies. Similarly attention needs to be given to the appropriate legal structures which take into account the aspirations to stakeholders: is a limited company the right vehicle? Should it be a public company? A cooperative, subsidiaries, branches? A European economic interest group? A European com-pany? Within the company different structures of corporate govern-ance may be more appropriate: to what extent should employee participation in decision-making be formalized, indeed structural-ized? All these issues are matters of the developing code of European company law, which all managers, not just company secretaries, should be aware of.

As part of the level playing field of the internal market programme, but also to assist in the development of cooperative and collaborative ventures the European Community has harmonized large parts of company law, and developed new legal structures for organizations trading in Europe.

The EC company law programme was started in the 1960s (and

indeed some contentious directives have remained in draft ever since) with the aim of stimulating mobility of enterprises and ensuring freedom of establishment. As the programme developed, it became more ambitious and now seeks to provide a coherent and holistic code of company law. In recent years it has also succumbed to political pressures to build a social dimension into a corporate code of law.

The two new alternative structures, European Economic Interest Group (EEIG) and European Company (Societas Europaea – SE) are both aimed at organizations operating in more than one member state, and should be considered by all companies as part of their strategy. Each has its own particular advantages and drawbacks over a conventional limited company.

The European company statute has had something of a chequered history, and remains in draft. The aim of the statute is to provide a pan-European framework of company law, to relieve companies of the burden of having to comply with different codes in different member states.

It is a purely voluntary mechanism whereby an SE can be formed by the merger of two or more companies from more than one member state, the formation of a holding company or a joint subsidiary. Wherever the SE operates it is governed by the statute, rather than the national law of whichever member state it is in. The statute covers most areas of company law, including rights of share-

Table 14.1 EC company law directives

1 Information to be published by companies and methods of disclosure
2 Company capitalization
3 Mergers and employee protection
4 Company accounts
5 Company structures
6 Division of public limited liability companies
7 Company group accounts
8 Auditors' qualifications
9 Consolidation of group accounts
10 Cross-border mergers
11 Disclosure requirements of branches
12 Single member private limited companies
13 Takeovers

Insider dealing
Disclosure of significant shareholding
European economic interest groups
European company statute
Partnerships
Undertakings for collective investment in transferable securities
Bank branches
Bank accounts

holders, general meetings, annual accounts, audits etc. Not covered are winding up and insolvency provisions. The statute has failed, therefore, to provide a single cohesive code of company law. In practice, SEs will still have to operate in tandem with the existing company laws of member states. Its appeal to many businesses is strictly limited, with many businessmen believing that any benefits to be derived are far outweighed by the resulting red tape and complexities. The statute is accompanied by a directive on employee involvement in decision-making, which requires all SEs to include a structure for employee involvement. Companies must choose between four different models, a one-tier board with employee directors; a two-tier system of a management board and a supervisory board with employee directors; a works council; or some other structure which is equivalent to the other three. Many UK companies have rejected the option of becoming an SE because of these provisions, believing that they introduce inflexibilities and rigidities which are unwarranted. Nevertheless there are considerable fiscal incentives to the establishment of a European company. This will be of particular use in setting up new ventures in different member states in allowing start-up costs and losses to be off-set efficiently against operating profits in another member state.

The option of becoming a European company is not limited to large companies. The threshold has been deliberately set so as to allow the participation of SMEs. A European company must have a market capitalization of just 100,000 ecus.

Based on the French notion of a *groupement d'intérêt économique* the European Economic Interest Group is similar to an SE, but does not codify the structures to quite the same extent. It is a new legal framework designed to encourage cross-border collaboration and cooperation in a simple and easy manner. The EEIG can be set up by two or more businesses operating in more than one member state. It must be wholly owned by those businesses. It is not restricted to limited liability companies, and can be a useful vehicle for sole-traders or partnerships. The EEIG is not supposed to make profits in its own right (any profits it may make must be directly disbursed to the participants and taxed accordingly) but is a vehicle for shared service or professional activities, such as research, marketing, distribution. An EEIG does not need to be capitalized, but there is joint and several liability amongst its owners for any debts. This has proved to be a particularly popular structure for many professional types of business, such as legal practices, providing an appropriate vehicle for such things as shared office space. An EEIG could be set up to bring together several small partners across the Community to bid for large contracts for example. The processes are designed to be simple. An EEIG does not have to file accounts or make annual reports. All that is required is that a contract be drawn up between the participants, and the founding of the EEIG be reported in the *Official Journal*.

The EEIG has surprised the Commission in its popularity amongst professional practices, but it is eminently suitable as a vehicle for small organizations wishing to extend into new territories in tandem with other bodies, able to minimize costs by sharing ancillary services. It should not be the vehicle for a new venture itself, as it is restricted in its ability to own shares in other undertakings, may not employ more than 500 people, or have any influence over the management of the participants.

The EEIG is therefore a relatively simply mechanism which allows for cross-border collaboration and partnerships without the bureaucracy involved in a merger, or forming joint subsidiaries. It does not have any of the prescriptions for employee involvement which are contained in the European company statute.

A further development of relevance to the sole-trader will be the implementation of the 12th Company Law Directive allowing a single person to form a limited liability company. Until recently, under UK law, at least two people were required to form a company.

Most of the rest of EC company law falls under the internal market heading, and should be perceived by managers as relevant simply in terms of the need for compliance. It is typified by the Commission acting as a handicapper in harmonizing the legal framework in which companies operate throughout the Community. On the positive side, the requirements for more transparent reporting and a harmonized system of takeovers should be of direct benefit to UK companies who are used to open and competitive corporate affairs, and will welcome the lifting of obstacles to taking over foreign companies, after so many years of being taken over.

The First Directive[66] on disclosure of information is implemented in the UK by the Companies Act 1985, and forms the basis of requirements for companies to be registered with Companies House, and to file the Memorandum and Articles of Association, along with an annual report.

The Second Directive[67] relates to the formation of public limited liability companies, and introduced the acronym PLC into the UK. Public companies in the EC must have a capitalization of at least 25,000 ecus, although member states may set a higher threshold. The directive, implemented by the Companies Act covers issuance of new shares, reduction in capital, dividends, liabilities, and puts restrictions on companies buying or financing third parties to buy their own shares.

The Third Directive[68] regulates merger activity between companies in one member state, and deals with both takeovers and mergers to form a new company. It specifies the contents of reports to be drawn up by the management of both companies, and provides minimum levels of protection for shareholders, creditors and employees.

The Fourth Directive[69] defines the contents and publication of annual accounts, to allow comparability throughout the Community.

It specifies the needs for auditing, allowing certain exemptions for SMEs.[70]

The Fifth Directive,[71] after more than twenty years in draft, has yet to be adopted in the face of continuing controversy over proposals for employee participation in decision-making. It is now into its third major redraft and covers the structure of public limited liability companies. In many aspects its provisions are similar to those of the European company statute. The directive would apply to all companies with 1,000 or more employees working within the Community and deals with the functions of company boards, liability of directors, conduct of general meetings, determination of dividends, and the functions of the auditor. It proposes similar options for a single-tier or two-tier structure of management as the SE detailed above. Additionally the directive would give employees or their representatives the right to a quarterly written report on the activities of the organization, the draft annual accounts and report, special reports as requested, and information on major decisions such as closures, mergers, takeovers and redundancies. This proposal has been one of the most contentious, and is a good example of an area where many businessmen, particularly those in the UK, feel that the Commission has stepped beyond the bounds of its competence into an area which should be the preserve of management.[72]

The Sixth Directive[73] or 'Scission Directive' governs the procedures to be followed where a company is wound-up but not liquidated, in cases where it is split up and sold-off. Similar in nature to the Third Directive it seeks to provide protection to shareholders, creditors and employees.

The Seventh Directive[74] complements the Fourth Directive dealing with group accounts and provides the basis for the consolidation of accounts of parent and subsidiary companies. Significantly it also provides a legal definition of a subsidiary, which has significant fiscal as well as fiduciary implications for many companies. The development of subsidiaries through acquisition is one of the most favoured strategies of UK companies seeking to enter new markets in the EC.

The Eighth Directive[75] defines who is qualified to carry out an audit of company accounts. Broadly speaking auditors must be graduates who have had three years practical training, and have passed an appropriate exam of professional competence.

The Ninth Directive remains in draft, principally due to the opposition of the UK government and British businesses who feel that it represents unwarranted interference in the management of companies, attempts to prescribe in law the formal relationships between companies in a group.

The Tenth Directive, still in draft, would extend the Third and Sixth Directives to cross-border mergers. As with other measures in this area it again seeks to protect creditors, shareholders and employees. Its purpose is to ease the difficulties associated with

Table 14.2   Definition of a subsidiary

A company is considered a subsidiary if it fulfils one of the following conditions:
1   The parent undertaking holds a major of the shareholders' voting rights;
2   The parent undertaking has the right to appoint or remove a majority of members of the Board;
3   The majority of members of the Board are appointed by the parent.

cross-border mergers. Until it is adopted international take-overs in some member states, such as Germany, will remain almost impossible except under certain precise circumstances.

The **Eleventh Directive**[76] puts overseas branches of companies on a comparable footing with regard to their reporting requirements as locally incorporated subsidiaries. The decision as to whether to set up branches or subsidiaries is an important one which needs to take into account the various fiscal provisions, as well as the bureaucracy involved in filing separate accounts and reports.

The **Twelfth Directive**[77] enables a single individual to form a limited liability company, and thereby keep his or her own personal assets separate from those of the trading company, whilst enjoying the protection of limited liability without the need for cooperation from a partner.

The **Thirteenth Directive**, which has yet to be adopted, forms a significant part of competition policy, and controls takeovers. It is closely related to the merger control regulations, and seeks to harmonize legislation which currently allows for barriers to hostile takeovers. The draft sets out procedures to be followed, and will also regulate the extent to which such tactics as 'poison pills' can be used as a defence against hostile takeovers.

15 Products

Open competitive markets, with a much larger number of consumers will almost certainly have a direct impact on the type of products sold, and the methods of manufacture. At the same time manufacturers are having to contend with more global challenges such as population ageing, environmental responsibility, energy efficiency and IT awareness. All this within the framework of a new code of law which itself is stimulating large-scale sectoral industrial restructuring. Planning new products and production methods will never have been harder as the application of advanced technologies make whole sectors, let alone products, redundant in a matter of years, if not months.

Each industrial sector will face its own tests which are beyond the scope of this book to examine, but there are some common challenges to commerce and industry as a whole (including the service sector) resulting directly from operating in a single market.

The extent to which a single market generates the capacity for a homogeneous or a heterogeneous approach is open to considerable debate, and needs to be examined in the light of individual products. If the expected economies of scale are to be achieved, this should lead to the development of products which can be marketed throughout the European Community. In practice, such products are likely to be few. There are probably no more than a few dozen truly global products or services, successfully manufactured and sold around the world, and these (Coca Cola, Sony Walkman, IBM PCs, Hilton hotels, etc.) tend to be the exception rather than the rule. In Europe, the shelves of supermarkets and shops in Berlin are filled with a very different product range from those in Barcelona. Again, there are very few genuinely European products − Gillette razors is one example. Homogeneity in this context cannot mean selling identical products throughout the Community. Where then are the economies of scale and production to be derived?

Paradoxically the wider market means the reverse; a heightened heterogeneity. A large free market stimulates greater segmentation, product differentiation and consumer sophistication as a result of increased choice and competition. At the same time producers are having to meet the needs of shorter product life-cycles, shorter delivery lead times, smaller production runs, and higher quality standards.

The possibilities for niche products are greatly enhanced in a wider market as a direct result of its scale. Particular products, such as left-handed scissors, or bespoke services which may not have generated sufficient demand in a small marketplace, become feasible commercial propositions in the wider market of 340 million consumers. This principle operates across all types and sizes of industry. The development costs of digital telephone exchanges mean that they need to be sold in more than one country to be recouped; the production costs of top of the range cars similarly demand large markets. If you could only sell one item per hundred thousand consumers, it is unlikely that in a market of say 60 million consumers, the ability to sell 600 items would make it a worthwhile venture. If you could sell 3,400 such items, the degree of customization, particularization and specialization required may well be worthwhile. The growth in niche marketing is expected to continue to boom as the market develops. Technological advances appropriately implemented allow for the development of niche products at the same time as mass marketing methods. T-shirt manufacturers have, for example, benefited from the development of hot-press technology which allows a myriad of designs to be printed, at relatively low cost, on to mass-produced T-shirts. Short runs of T-shirts for a particular occasion or event become economically feasible.

Product differentiation is a vital component to comparative advantage. If all goods supplied in the same marketplace were (or appeared to be) essentially the same, the determinant of competitiveness would be solely price. Differentiation can be arrived at through many means from innovation and product design, through to advertising and packaging, quality of performance, delivery and service. The increasing sophistication of consumers demands a mix of all possible differentiators to be applied.

Of course, the increase in size of market is countered by the increase in number of competitors. This stimulates a heightened requirement for product differentiation if the competitive edge is to be developed and sustained. Your washing powder has to be continually ahead of other competitors if consumers are to be persuaded to buy it. Product differentiation has proved increasingly difficult in such competitive areas as car manufacture where the product itself has become more homogeneous (particularly since the oil shock), and the challenges for manufacturers are to build in differences in the design ranging from colour to the accessories.

This heightened differentiation in turn helps to educate a more sophisticated and demanding consumer. Greater levels of education, a mushrooming of travel and experience, and increased choice has led to a higher degree of discernment in purchasing decisions. At the same time consumers have adopted remarkably diverse life-styles which too need to be accommodated in product design. The growth of the fast-food and convenience foods market, for example, have been a direct response to the increasing number of women in the labour market. The development of so-called eco-products, similarly respond to an increasingly better-educated and demanding consumer. Greater awareness of health, safety and social issues by individuals needs to be catered for. Young people in Europe are more aware than ever before of the processes by which products reach them, in particular the potential for environmental damage. Such a level of sophistication needs to be understood early on in the production process – products will no longer be able to compete on price difference alone.

Neither should producers be fooled by 'Je suis européen' type slogans. Culturally, physically, and climatically the European Community will remain eclectic. Cultural differences between member states, and indeed regions of the Community will not be erased, or even levelled. Political pressures mitigating against wider federalism may even themselves stimulate greater cultural diversity. Appreciation of the miscellany within the relatively small territory of the Community must go beyond simple differentiation of marketing products, and tends to extend right back into product development and design.

Climatic differences are probably fairly obvious. A manufacturer of leisure wear, for example, is bound to sell more T-shirts in the south, and more sweaters in the north. However, there are other significant product differences throughout the Community which are appropriate to particular regions or countries. In less densely populated countries, for example, where land is not at such a premium, houses tend to be bigger. For these reasons, washing machines do not need to be as space-saving as in the UK. Most washing machines sold in Germany are, for example, top-loaders, rather than front-loaders. The cultural rejection of men carrying handbags in the north of Europe means that men's clothes need to have more pockets if they are aimed at the Danish, UK or German markets, than those items aimed at the Mediterranean markets. Each product needs to be carefully examined to see whether it is appropriate for each particular marketplace. BMW, for example, has developed its distinctive product with a common marketing theme but a very highly differentiated product throughout the Community. This has considerable implications for its production techniques. In its home market the larger models (5 and 7 series saloon cars), with powerful engines are at a premium (probably something to do with the lack of speed limits on motorways in Germany); it therefore does not market the 5 or 7 series with engines of less than 2 litre capacity. However, it produces a 1.8 litre version, especially for the UK where performance is not rated so highly. Production managers and product designers will need to focus carefully on manufacturing systems which are flexible enough to produce a number of different designs of essentially the same product on the same assembly lines. To use again the example of the washing machine manufacturer seeking to trade in both Germany and the UK, two separate assembly lines to put together the basic components in a different shape would not be efficient. Somehow the same assembly line should be able to cope with front and top loaders with the minimum of inconvenience, re-tooling or down-time.

Customizing products to meet market, and individual consumer needs is probably the most important technique being adopted by manufacturers in the single market. There are, of course, many different approaches to this. Several Japanese car manufacturers for example, believe that one of the keys to competitiveness in the UK is the number of accessories that are fitted to a car. They have accordingly produced cars which are full of gadgets as standard. An opposite approach has been taken by the Ford Motor Company. Recognizing the same thing, it has designed cars which are able to take several hundred different additional accessories, or modifications. Excluding colour, there are more than a million different types of Ford Sierra covering the various combinations of additions: with or without sun-roofs, power steering, electric windows and so on. To do this it has had to invest in and develop some of the most advanced flexible manufacturing systems in the world which are capable of delivering single customized cars at the press of a few buttons in response to individual customers' requirements.

Product life-cycles have for decades been getting shorter and shorter. The only impact of the single market on this process is to speed it up. More than twenty years ago a study of product life cycles[78] revealed 55 per cent of all the products on sale in US supermarkets did not exist ten years previously. Many of these products are likely to be simply fashionable items which were never expected to be on the market for long, but in the huge growth sectors such as electronics, the life-cycle of a new product is shortening rapidly in the face of a tide of technological advance. From the demise of the slide-rule upon the invention of the pocket calculator, IT products have been developing at such a rate that it is likely that a computer bought today is already obsolete within a few months in terms of price as well as performance.

Producers competing in such markets will find responsiveness to technological advances the key to sustained growth, but will face enormous challenges in constantly updating and developing new products. There is no room for complacency. Innovation will be examined in Chapter 19, but the implications of fast changing products and ever shortening life-cycles will be felt in R & D budgets, in the need to cooperate with others on product development, and in concentrations of core activities. The development of EC-wide technical standards should do much to mitigate the rapid changes in product development. If R & D costs are to be recovered then producers will need to have confidence that the product will not just be able to function across the territories of the single market, but will also be compatible with future developments. The convergence of information technology with home entertainment technology for example, requires a uniform standard to allow producers of, say, video recorders to design them so that they will interface in the future with personal computers. Designers of washing machines must build in the capacity for them to be controlled electronically, even remotely, by automated home management systems. The pace of change cannot be underestimated. The Digital Music Interface (MIDI) which brings together keyboard synthesizers with computers and sound samplers is a relatively new development, but one which heralds massive changes for a whole range of consumer equipment. Facsimile machines, which have not been commercially available for much more than ten years are already verging on the obsolete unless they can communicate directly with other office equipment such as scanners, photo-copiers, and word processors. The development of multi-media communications and technologies either at work, or in the home, is a prime example of the need for producers to be alert to the pace of change, the possibilities for differentiation and customization (and therefore short manufacturing runs), and the necessity for collaboration and cooperation at a pre-competitive stage.

The commercial imperatives of being involved with the development of, and conforming with, technical standards are no less important than the importance of conforming with and anticipating European standards for health and safety, environmental and consumer protection as well as the imperative of meeting the highest of quality standards.

16 Human resources management

As we saw in Chapter 9, the social dimension to the European Community is a fast developing one. The main issues identified so far have been questions of management flexibility, compliance costs, the effects on competitiveness, and the management of industrial relations. More specifically however, managing the human resource aspect of trading in Europe concerns issues of recruitment and retention, training and education, on top of employment conditions, protection and health and safety.

Most proposed European legislation concerned with harmonization of various aspects of employment protection remains in draft having been hotly contested over many years. In particular that relating to a flexible workforce is subject to compromise and fudge. Nevertheless they cannot be ignored by UK managers. The opt-out from the social protocol, the refusal to sign the Social Charter, and more particularly, for example, the derogation from the directive on part-time work should be seen at one level by any cautious manager as being temporary. At a practical level such devices can only be regarded as unsustainable. In developing Europe-wide strategies it is a nonsense that any company can maintain widely divergent employment conditions across the Community within the same workforce. Legislation already agreed covers redundancy and equal treatment (including pensions). Nearly all remaining employment protection law in the UK serves to implement these directives. Their implications are only recently being fully understood, and their impacts are wide reaching.

The Social Charter which lays the basis for the Social Action Programme forms the framework for future developments in the Community for which managers need to be prepared. (The social protocol is merely an enabling mechanism.) Apart from the implications of compliance costs and inherent rigidities and inflexibilities, managers need to be aware that the principles laid down in the charter are being followed by managers in other parts of the Community. Whether operating at home or in another member state the expectations of the workforce are conditioned by these principles, with consequent impacts for competition for skilled labour. Many managers have also put forward the view that the principles of the social charter all represent good management practice in any case, and it is only the inflexible nature of proposals for putting them into practice put forward by the Commission which are likely to cause problems. The Social Charter calls upon member states, and therefore employers to address:

- **Improvement of living and working conditions**
  Approximation of working conditions throughout the Community, in particular the organization and flexibility of working hours; the establishment of a minimum working week; and upward harmonization of the rights of those in non-typical patterns of works.
- **Right to freedom of movement**
  The right to freedom of movement implies further rights to social security and tax advantages for those working and their families, as well as the non-employed.
- **Employment and remuneration**
  Rights to a fair wage, either by law or collective agreement. (It should be noted that there is no move towards establishing a minimum wage.)
- **Rights to social protection**
  All workers should be covered by social security cover in proportion to their length of service, to the pay they receive, and their contributions.
- **Right to freedom of association and collective bargaining**
  Every employer and worker should have the right to belong freely to the professional and trade union organization of their choice. This entails the right to conclude collective agreements, to resort to collective action (including the right to strike). It also includes the right not to belong to a trade union without any personal or professional harm.
- **Right to vocational training**
  Every worker should have the right to continue his vocational training throughout his working life. Member states should set up schemes whereby every citizen can undergo retraining to improve his skills, or acquire new skills.
- **Right of men and women to equal treatment**
  Equal opportunities and equal treatment for men and women must be guaranteed.
- **Right to information, consultation and worker participation**
  Information, consultation and worker participation should be developed along appropriate lines and in such a way as to take account of the level provisions, contractual agreements and practices in force in member states.
- **Right to health protection and safety at the workplace**
  Every worker should enjoy satisfactory health and safety conditions at his place of work, and steps should be take to harmonize health and safety measures upwards.

As has been mentioned, much of the extant UK employment protection legislation implements directives already adopted at a European level. Abolition of the closed shop, for example, while fully in line with government policies, was necessary in order to comply with the freedom of establishment. The Community has a clear intention to develop the existing code in a number of areas in much greater detail. The directives already agreed, and those in process are set out below. It cannot be sufficiently stressed that the UK opt-out of the Social Chapter, and its refusal to sign the Social Charter, should not be seen by managers operating on a European scale as much more than a technicality. Compliance with most of this legislation will be necessary throughout most of the rest of the Community. Businesses' awareness and involvement in the development of the code should continue, if managers are to be sufficiently prepared.

Redundancies

The 1975 directive on collective redundancies, implemented in the UK through the 1975 Employment Protection Act, and 1978 Employment Protection Consolidation Act, as well as the transfer of undertakings regulations, calls for preliminary consultation with employees, with a view to mitigating the circumstances, and notification of the intended redundancies to a competent authority. It applies to private sector organizations seeking to make redundant more than 10 people in firms where 20 to 100 are employed, 10 per cent in organizations with up to 300 employed, and more than thirty where there are more than 300 people employed. The Commission intends to extend the directive to cover individual redundancies, but this is likely to be progressed under the Social Protocol, and may be avoided within the United Kingdom. It will, however, bear a particular relevance to companies using the strategy of merger and acquisition in Europe, who will have to comply with all legislation in this area in taking over the existing commitments of employers.

Relevant directives adopted by the Council are:

- The approximation of the laws of member states relating to collective redundancies[79]
- The approximation of the laws of member states relating to the safeguarding of employees' rights in the event of transfers of undertakings, businesses or parts of businesses[80]
- The approximation of the laws of member states relating to the protection of employees in the event of the insolvency of their employer.[81]

Equal treatment

The treaty requires member states to enforce the principle of equal pay. Various directives and ECJ judgments have broadened the scope of the treaty. Broadly there are six equal treatment directives:

- The approximation of the laws of the member states relating to the application of the principle of equal pay for men and women[82]
- Implementation of the principle of equal treatment for men and women as regards access to employment, vocational training and promotion and working conditions[83]
- The progressive implementation of the principle of equal treatment for men and women in matters of social security
- Implementation of the principle of equal treatment for men and women in matters of occupational social security[84]
- Application of the principle of equal treatment between men and women engaged in an activity, including agriculture, in a self-employed capacity, and on the protection of self-employed women during pregnancy and motherhood[85]
- Changing the burden of proof in cases of sex discrimination (still in draft).

Interpretation of these various directives is still unfolding in different courts and tribunals throughout the Community. However, they generally require equal pay for men and women, regardless of marital status 'for the same work, or for work to which equal value is attributed'. The definition of 'pay' is uncertain ground, but should be taken to include all forms of remuneration and benefits including holidays, and more problematically, pensions. Much of the legislation has been implemented in the UK through the Equal Pay Act, and the two Sex Discrimination Acts.

The Equal Pay Act did, however, deliberately exclude pensions. The EC State Social Security Directive requires member states to eliminate all discrimination on grounds of sex in statutory schemes which provide protection against old age, sickness, invalidity, unemployment and accidents at work. Although a 1985 European Court of Justice judgment forced the UK into equalizing retirement ages, the UK has yet to equalize pension ages. This is, however, only a temporary derogation and all member states are obliged to equalize their pensionable ages as soon as possible. A Green Paper on the subject was published by the DHSS in 1985 proposing a flexible decade of retirement, probably pivoting around 62 or 63. Equal retirement and pension ages already exist in Denmark, France, Germany and The Netherlands. So long as the state scheme continues to be discriminatory, occupational pension schemes may also discriminate in terms of benefits and contributions. Implementation of the Occupational Schemes Directive was due by the end of 1992, but in practice has already been put into effect by the judgement in the cases of Barber v. Guardian Royal Exchange,[86] and Marshall v. Southampton Area Health Authority. In practical terms this Directive will change UK pension schemes considerably, following the enormous amount of reform that has been introduced during the last five years anyway. Although actuarial considerations may be taken into account when assessing benefits, there is a clear cost implication of introducing such changes as widowers' benefits. The position has, unfortunately changed considerably over a number of years following various court cases, and may well continue to change, as most cases seem to be being decided in favour of the claimant.

A significant development will be the adoption of the draft directive on the burden of proof. As well as going against the tradition of UK legislation, and assuming that the employer is guilty until proven innocent in cases of sex discrimination, the current draft includes a clear definition of indirect discrimination which goes well beyond that already in UK law:

> Where an apparently neutral provision, criterion or practice dispro-portionately disadvantages the members of one sex, by reference in particular to marital or family status, and is not objectively justified by a necessary reason or condition unrelated to the sex of the person concerned.

Because more than four in five UK part-time workers are women, any 'apparently neutral provision' which treats part-time workers differently from full-time workers – such as access to a company pension scheme – would be considered indirect discrimination, irrespective of intent.

Flexible working patterns

Whilst there is agreement within the Community that flexible working patterns – part-time and temporary work, job-sharing etc. as well as measures to encourage women to work – are pragmatic solutions to both unemployment and shortages of labour, the UK and the rest of the Community have differed on the best approach to encourage such developments. In the UK there has been substantial deregulation and removal of employment protection from 'peripheral' workers in order to encourage employers to take on part-time workers. The Commission, on the other hand, believes that increasing the level of protection will encourage individuals to take up new patterns of work.

Part-time work

The 1992 Directive on Voluntary Part-time Work establishes the principle that all part-time workers should receive the same treatment as full-time workers in the same situation. This would apply to ordinary basic wage or salary, and any other consideration, whether in cash or kind which the worker receives from his employment, including health and safety, fringe benefits, pension schemes, pro-tection from dismissal, rights to time off for union or public duties, and holidays, and to be included in any consultative procedures which are established.

Temporary work

Amended in 1984 the draft directive on the supply of temporary workers by temporary employment businesses and fixed-duration contracts of employment, was also raised under Article 100, and seems destined never to be adopted. As currently drafted it regulates temporary employment agencies, but also puts an end to liability on user-undertakings for remuneration and social security payments if the agency defaults.

The existing draft would also give temporary employees pro-rata rights as full-time employees to facilities the organization offers, and would also limit fixed-duration contracts to three months, renewable to six months only, unless the temporary worker is covering for someone on parental leave.

Parental leave

Whilst the maternity leave provisions in UK law are well established, parental leave, including paternity leave is at the discretion of individual employers, about a third of whom have some form of parental leave. This draft directive would give all wage-earning parents of either sex, regardless of marital status, the right to return to work after a break to look after a child of three months. This would follow on from maternity leave. There would also be a minimum number of days a year an employee could take off for pressing family reasons such as a wedding of a child, or death of a near relative. Eight member states currently have parental leave provisions. Estimates of cost will vary according to the profile of employees within an organization, but it is assumed that around 1 per cent of males and 2 per cent of females would take parental leave in any one year.

Continuous education and training

Also included within the Draft Charter of Minimum Social Rights is the proposal that every worker shall have the opportunity to continue his vocational training during his working life. It is proposed that the public authorities, enterprises, and where appropriate, the two sides of industry shall set up continuing and permanent training systems enabling every citizen to undergo retraining to improve his skills or acquire new skills, particularly in the light of technical developments.

This proposal takes up the theme of a 1986 Council Resolution, and 1987 Commission Report which underlined the need to reinforce continuous training for wage-earners as an investment. It is believed that adequate training policies which anticipate the future will multiply the effects of material investment and improve results as regards productivity and work organization. The main thrust of the Community's approach is that the training of workers should not be left entirely to the public authorities, and that employers need to take a more active part in this type of training. (In the UK we see this with the development of the Training and Enterprise Councils (TECs), Chambers of Commerce, and One-Stop Shops.) This recognizes that in-service training and a skilled workforce are the prerequisites for success. Such an investment will significantly improve the competitiveness of productivity of the firm, and there is no conflict between the firm's interests and those of the employee as regards the importance of training.

The Community sees its role in this area as threefold:

- exploiting the experience gained with a view to transfer and dissemination
- developing new products and methods of training
- promoting the development of new in-service training practices.

To this end the Community has now adopted a medium term action programme for vocational training to implement these themes. Further action in this area can be anticipated which may include legislation on training leave; on tax allowances (the UK is alone in not allowing employees a tax allowance for any training materials they personally buy); and on the recognition of qualifications acquired through primarily 'in-house' training.

Employee participation

Employee participation in decision making of companies is widespread, mandatory and for the most part institutionalized throughout the Community, apart from in the United Kingdom. Various attempts have been made to harmonize practice, and the current outlook remains uncertain, and clouded by debate on the legal basis of European legislation in this area.

Companies examining their employment policies should have an eye to the possible legislative requirements which may have to be implemented within the UK, but should also consider the diversity of practice throughout the Community if establishing Europe-wide operations.

Setting aside health and safety legislation two European directives calling for employee participation have been adopted by the Council, and a further six proposals adopted by the Commission, with others being put forward. The implemented directives are:

Approximation of laws relating to collective redundancies

Agreed in 1975 and implemented in 1977 this directive is covered in the UK by the 1975 Employment Protection Act, and the 1978 Employment Protection (Consolidation) Act. It requires consultation with representatives of employees where an employer is contemplating redundancies, with a view to avoiding and reducing the number of dismissals.

The acquired rights directive

Agreed in 1977 this directive has been implemented in the UK though the Transfer of Undertakings (Protection of Employment) Regulations, 1981, and ensures that employee rights are transferred to the new owner of the business. It also calls for employee representatives to be consulted about the transfer before the event.

Proposals adopted by the Commission which are at various points in the legislative process, and stand varying chances of being adopted in the face of a lack of agreement between member states are:

Draft fifth company law directive on the structure of PLCs

In its currently amended form, this would apply to PLCs with 1,000 or more employees. Member states would have to choose between four options for employee participation within companies:

1   A two-tier board — one 'supervisory' and one 'executive' where between one third and one half of the supervisory board must be employee representatives with the same rights to information as any other director.
2   A single-tier board of directors with a minority of employee directors.
3   A body representing employees (such as a works council), which would have a right to be consulted on the administration, situation, progress and prospects of the company, its competitive position, its credit situation and investment plans. The works council would have the same rights to information as the supervisory directors.
4   Any system established by collective agreements which would make provision for employee participation at a supervisory level.

Under whichever option is chosen employee representatives would have the same information rights as shareholder representatives to receive a quarterly written report on the activities of the organization; the draft annual accounts and report; special reports as requested; information on major decisions such as closures, mergers, takeovers and redundancies.

This draft directive has been strongly opposed by the UK, but under the Single European Act it cannot be vetoed by one country alone. Debate continues on the legal status of the draft. It is however an important part of the company law programme, and forms the bedrock of EC proposals for employee participation.

Draft ninth company law directive on the conduct of groups containing subsidiaries

This draft introduces the concept of a 'control contract' which gives legal status to the power to manage a group and requires the company's control contract to be approved by the 'supervisory body' of the company, along the lines of the draft Fifth Directive.

Draft tenth company law directive on cross-border mergers of PLCs

Designed to facilitate cross-border mergers this draft deals with protection of creditors and employees, and contains significant and substantive references to the draft Fifth Directive.

Draft European company statute

The purpose of the statute is to provide a system of law which is independent of national law to encourage cross-frontier cooperation. The provisions for employee participation are similar to those of the Fifth Directive, although it will be up to individual companies to choose an option, rather than member states. It also allows companies the option not to introduce structures for participation if employees do not want them. The option to become a European company will be voluntary.

All the company law directives form part of the original internal market programme and may not be subject to veto by one member state.

Draft directive on procedures for informing and consulting employees (the 'Vredeling' directive)

Whilst this draft has now been effectively blocked, it is worth noting, as its provisions are likely to re-emerge as another draft directive under the Charter of Minimum Social Rights. It would apply to all companies with 1,000 or more employees in the Community, and would require management to provide a clear picture of the activities of the parent and subsidiary organizations, including details of structure, economic and financial situation, the probable

development of the production and sales, employment and investment prospects and trends. One of the most contentious provisions
is the right of employee representatives to bypass local management
if they are not satisfied with the information they are being provided.

On top of the information rights, employee representatives would
have a right to be consulted on closures or transfer, restrictions or
modifications in the activities of the company, major modifications
with regard to working practices (especially in connection with the
introduction of new technologies), and any long-term cooperation
with other undertakings. The current draft, unlike the Fifth Directive,
does allow management to withhold information which could sub-
stantially damage the undertaking's commercial interests.

Practice in member states generally reflects the provisions set out
in the Fifth Directive. In The Netherlands employee participation
revolves around both supervisory boards and works councils. Every
limited liability company with more than 100 employees is required
to have a supervisory board. Companies with more than 35
employees must have a works council. Smaller companies must
hold at least six monthly meetings with employees.

In Germany one third of the members of a supervisory board
must be employee representatives (one half in companies with
more than 2,000 employees). Supervisory boards tend to operate on
a consensual basis. France has a system of works councils which
have only limited influence on decision-making, but must be
informed and consulted on major decisions. The works council also
has a small level of funding to spend on social and cultural activities.
Belgium too has a system of works councils. In this case they have
the power to fix the dates of the annual holidays. In Portugal and
Spain bodies representing employees at a company level are elected
by workers and must have access to information necessary to exercise
a democratic say in the activities of the company.

The level of financial participation in the rest of Europe is relatively
small compared to the UK. The Commission has, however, adopted
a Recommendation on the development of financial participation
expressing its desirability, and some elements of good practice
based upon their own researches (the Pepper Report).

Uncertainty remains the principal problem facing businesses
planning employment policies for 1992, when trying to account for
legislation. It is overall, a political and institutional question, whether
or not the foregoing proposals will come to be implemented. However, it is useful to note that, apart from the right to collective
bargaining, there is not a single International Labour Organization
(ILO) convention ratified − let alone implemented − by all the
member states of the Community (see Table 16.1).

Table 16.1 Ratification of ILO conventions

	B	DK	G	GR	E	F	IRL	I	L	NL	P	UK
Labour clauses (public contracts)	X	X			X	X		X		X		
Right to collective bargaining	X	X	X	X	X	X	X	X	X		X	X
Discrimination in respect of employment and occupation	X	X	X	X	X	X		X		X	X	
Protection of workers against ionizing radiation	X	X	X	X	X	X		X		X		X
Guarding of machinery					X			X				
Hygiene in commerce and offices	X	X	X		X	X		X			X	X
Minimum wage fixing					X	X			X			
Annual holidays with pay			X		X		X	X	X	X		
Accommodation of crews		X				X		X	X			X
Prevention of accidents (seafarers)		X	X	X	X	X	X					
Workers' representatives		X	X		X	X		X	X	X	X	X
Dock work					X	X		X		X	X	
Benzene			X	X	X	X		X				
Minimum age for employment			X	X	X		X	X	X	X		
Occupational cancer		X	X				X					
Rural workers' organizations	X	X	X		X	X		X		X		X
Paid educational leave		X			X	X				X		X
Human resources development		X	X		X	X	X	X		X	X	X
Migrant workers								X		X		
Tripartite consultation	X	X	X	X	X	X	X	X		X	X	X
Continuity of employment (seafarers)					X	X		X		X	X	
Annual paid leave (seafarers)					X	X		X		X	X	
Merchant shipping (minimum standards)	X	X	X	X	X	X		X	X	X	X	X
Working environment, pollution, noise, vibration			X		X	X				X		X
Nursing personnel		X				X		X		X		
Conditions of employment in the public service		X			X			X			X	X
Promotion of collective bargaining					X							
Safety and health of workers					X						X	
Workers with family responsibilities					X						X	
Maintenance of rights in social security					X							
Termination of employment					X							
Employment of handicapped persons			X	X								

Freedom of establishment and movement

The freedom of movement and establishment is a key part of the programme to complete the internal market, that involves geographical mobility, rights of residence and work, rights to acquire land, and the recognition of qualifications. Migration between member states, especially by professional workers remains small. The most recent figures suggest that there are currently 398,000 immigrant employees (mostly from Ireland) from the rest of the Community in the UK (1.9 per cent of the working population), whilst there are 81,000 UK citizens employed in other member states, more than a third of whom are in West Germany. Only about 5 million of the 340 million citizens of the Community are living in member states which are not their own. This is less than 2 per cent and is about a tenth of the degree of mobility between States in the United States. It is significant to note at this early stage that the levels of migration that do exist follow a clear trend of mobility from the periphery towards the centre of the Community. The Irish into the United Kingdom, Southern Italians into France, Belgium and Germany, Portuguese into France, Greeks into Germany, Spanish into France. There is a negligible flow in the opposite direction (with the sole exception of UK nationals moving to Spain).[87]

The Treaty of Rome lays down the fundamental principle of freedom of movement: 'The abolition of any discrimination based on nationality between workers of the member states as regards employment, remuneration and other conditions of work and employment' (Article 48(2)). Further articles cover the right to accept offers of employment, to move freely within the Community for this purpose, and to remain in a member state after having been employed there. Article 51 provides that necessary measures are taken in the field of social security. Freedom of establishment, defined as 'the right to take up and pursue activities as self-employed persons and to set up and manage firms' is guaranteed by Article 52.

However, in just the same way as barriers to trade in goods have sought to protect national industries, many and varied means have been used to prevent foreign workers and professionals from working or practising outside of their home country. These have included, for example, Belgium's refusal to allow additional leave to those foreign nationals required to do military service; ski instructors in Italy must be Italian; equal treatment in Luxembourg has not been guaranteed for children of other countries; freedom to work did not apply to part-timers in The Netherlands; the German tax system did not allow for rebates in the case of EC workers' children living abroad; in the United Kingdom the provision of local authority housing subsidies discriminates against non UK EC nationals. In Greece foreigners are not allowed to buy certain designated areas which constitute about half of the country. In France any lawyer can practise, so long as he is in partnership with a French national who must complete and sign-off any work. The list of restrictions is endless, but has served to distort the labour market in such a way that, for example, whilst certain education authorities in the UK suffer a severe shortage of primary and secondary school teachers,

Irish qualified teachers (of whom there are a surplus) have not been able to work as teachers in the UK on the grounds of a lack of local authority housing!

The ability to recruit and attract labour throughout the Community will be a key element to any organization's strategy in combating the effects of demographic change in the UK, and any ensuing skill shortages. Conversely it may aggravate the situation, if skilled emigration from the UK rises to the proportions currently being suffered by Ireland, as a consequence of generally low wage rates, climate and other factors, such as availability of accommodation, influencing individuals' decisions on where they choose to work.

Various aspects of completing the market can be expected to stimulate an increase in cross-border migration. Company law designed to encourage intra-community cooperation; the opening up of public contracts; and the various Community R & D collaboration programmes (Esprit, Race, Brite etc.).

As well as the different education programmes to encourage the mobility of students and young people, the Community has agreed several measures to ensure the rights of workers and their families geographical and occupational mobility as well as social integration. The treaty itself guarantees that any national of a member state may leave his country of origin, enter and stay in another member state in order to look for and take up gainful employment. In different judgments the European Court of Justice has ruled that this applies to part-time workers, to jobs in the public service, and to certain 'extra-Community' countries. Regulations have ensured the application of a single body of legislation affecting legal cases involved with social security; the conservation of any acquired rights (employment, residence, social security etc.); and equal treatment between nationals and citizens of other member states. The Community is in the process of dealing with other aspects including the free movement of pensioners, but probably the most significant development is the agreement on mutual recognition of professional qualifications.

Up until 1987 efforts had been made to harmonize qualifications in specific vocational areas. As a consequence of this work different directives dealing with architects, insurance brokers, lawyers, nurses, dentists, vets, midwives, pharmacists and hairdressers have been agreed. These have been a long time in the legislative process. (The architects' directive took twelve years' to agree, a directive dealing with engineers has been 'on the table' before the Council of Ministers since May 1969!) Clearly this approach would never have made a significant impact on the European labour force as a whole.

The so-called 'new approach' is a system of recognition of higher education diplomas for occupational purposes. Abandoning the efforts to coordinate training courses, the system relies on mutual confidence between member states and the principle of comparability of training. It ensures (with certain exceptions) that a national of

Table 16.2   Mutual recognition of qualifications

- Wholesale trade and intermediaries in commerce, industry and small craft industries (64/222)
- Industry and small craft industries (64/427)
- Retail trade (68/364)
- Self-employed persons in personal service (68/368)
- Food manufacturing and beverage industries (68/366)
- Wholesale coal industry (70/523)
- Toxic products trade (74/556)
- Doctors (75/362)
- Itinerant activities (75/369)
- Insurance agents and brokers (77/92)
- Lawyers (77/249)
- Nurses (77/452)
- Transport (77/796)
- Dental practitioners (78/686)
- Veterinary surgeons (78/1026)
- Midwives (80/154)
- Travel agents (82/470)
- Hairdressers (82/849)
- Architects (85/834)
- Pharmacists (85/433)

one member state who has acquired his qualification through no less than three years of training post-secondary school, can practise in another member state where this activity is subject to conditions concerning qualifications. The directive excludes individuals when in the exercise of official authority. It also permits member states to require those in the 'legal' professions (including accountants) to take an 'aptitude' test or undergo further training before they are accepted as being qualified.

Along with these measures to smooth over the bureaucratic and procedural problems associated with working in another member state, various rights to the families of migrant workers have been established by the European Court of Justice: spouses and dependants are similarly entitled to take up residence and paid employment − even if they are not Community nationals themselves.

With the opening of the Channel Tunnel we can expect to see an increase in the number of 'frontier-workers' − defined as anyone domiciled in one country to which he returns at least once a week, and working in a territory of another country. In most instances they are entitled to fiscal and social security benefits in both countries concerned.

The compliance impacts are therefore considerable, along with the implications of a highly mobile and competitive labour market. The management response to these developments is a crucial one. For most organizations, but particularly service sector companies, which account for more than threequarters of employment in the

UK, the ability to add value stems directly from the ability to attract, train, retrain, and develop the skills of the workforce. Within a leveller playing field, management of human resources is a much more important competitive edge.

Operating in a European context presents some obvious labour challenges – internationalization of skills such as languages, for example, but some more discrete strains from the top to the bottom of an organization: productivity levels in an organization, for so long masked by different exchange rates became glaringly obvious in competitive markets.

As we have seen when looking at corporate structures, employees will need to become more multi-functional, mobile within an organization, flexible to new situations, and adaptable to short-term project work. Such employees who also possess the necessary language skills, and cultural perspectives will be few and far between and competition for them is likely to be intense. That said, employers will have a far wider labour market from which to recruit, provided they do not limit their horizons to their own region or country, or to particular sections of the Community, or to particular modes of employment. The impacts of the development of trans-European communications networks, for example, make the question; 'Should I move the workforce to the work, or the work to the workforce?' a very real issue.

Identification of the necessary skills should be the first step for all managers – both for their own workforces and their own careers! A skills audit of the existing workforce is likely to reveal unexpected talents which could be exploited.

As should be clear by now, whether or not it forms part of the corporate strategy to operate in another member state (and it will probably only be the case for less than a quarter of all UK companies) the fact that organizations from overseas will be operating in their foreign markets, means that all organizations should consider themselves to be in an international market. There is therefore a need for an international perspective to recruitment. The United Kingdom has one of the most liberal employment regimes which affords employers considerable flexibility. This may not be the case in a number of other member states, and employers recruiting abroad need to be keenly aware of local labour laws (which may, for example,

Table 16.3   Human resource management implications

- Skills
- Management processes
- Patterns of work
- Productivity
- Organizational structures
- Internationalization

require consultation with local unions, or the involvement of local employment agencies).

An immediate question which needs to be faced in the internal labour market, whether at home or abroad, is the choice between indigenous local, or migrant expatriate labour. When operating abroad, local staff will have a closer knowledge of the market, and local trading conditions, as well as local contacts. They may not, however, fully understand the organization, will almost certainly require different employment conditions, and present greater problems for remote managers. Employing local staff, does however, have the added bonus of displaying a strong commitment to a new market. When operations are based at home, overseas staff introduce different skills, cultures and perspectives to the organization which adds to the richness of the organizational culture, but also enables a considerable widening or at least understanding of target markets.

Retention of staff is as important as recruitment. On average employees change employers six times through their working life. This has been a steadily rising rate, as individuals' own ambitions fail to be fulfilled in single organizations. Appropriately skilled individuals seeking a breadth of experience, a constant learning situation, and steadily increasing levels of responsibility find mobility as the better means to career progression. Employers will need to respond to these aspirations in order to be competitive in recruitment and retention. This is not simply a question of providing competitive pay rates (although this is important), but providing appropriate employment conditions for a flexible and diverse labour force. Maternity provisions, childcare, access for the disabled, flexible working patterns (yearly hours, part-time working, telecommuting, temporary or fixed-term contract staff), opportunities for training, suitable levels of employment protection, early breaks for new responsibilities are all keenly sought by skilled and mobile workers – and may be offered by competitors. There are, of course, considerable cost implications, but these may be recouped in productivity gains.

A survey of UK companies' responses to the human resource challenges of the single market reveals that for many organizations a fundamental root and branch review of structures, responsibilities, processes and supporting technologies is a matter of necessity.[88] Europeanization of management is a clear imperative.

Consistently over a number of years UK firms have rated skill shortages as a major constraint on output growth. According to business surveys carried out by the European Commission, recruitment difficulties throughout the Community have increased steadily with the exception of Ireland and Denmark. The biggest increases have occurred in the UK and the Golden Triangle countries. The patterns of skill shortages vary from country to country, and need to be borne in mind in making locational decisions where there is a human resource impact. In France, high demand will be for the liberal professions and technicians, whilst there is likely to be a low demand for unskilled and agricultural workers. In Germany one forecast predicts an increase of 3.4 million highly skilled jobs, and a decrease of 2 million unskilled jobs by 2010. In the UK there is likely to be a rapid growth in the employment of managers, and the demand for graduates is likely to be intensely competitive. The clear response for the Community, member states, and companies is to increase the output of training of both school leavers, but more importantly the existing labour force.

Community education programmes

The twin engines of change in the 1990s, information technology and the increased competition that will derive from completion of the internal market will, inevitably, whatever social arrangements are concluded, involve a dislocation of the labour market. With varying degrees of skill shortages and unemployment, management of human resources as a competitive weapon will become increasingly important. Whilst it is known that the majority of the those who will be at work by the year 2010 are already at work, still insufficient attention is paid to the retraining of those in work. Of the 340 million people in the Community, more than a fifth are currently in primary, secondary, higher or further education. For the first time ever, the 1992 undergraduate intake into British universities had a majority of mature students, rather than school-leavers. Community programmes to encourage mobility of students, collaboration and exchanges of information go far beyond a simple call for a 'People's Europe'. They provide a rich resource and a wealth of talent for those recruiting their European managers and workforces into the 1990s.

In tandem with the Community's various research programmes Esprit, Brite, RACE, Sprint, and Eureka, as well as Delta (which encourages the use of new technologies in schools and universities), are the education programmes. Community involvement in education does not stretch to harmonizing the way students are taught, nor the education they receive. (The Lingua programme, providing funds aimed at encouraging students throughout the Community to learn two foreign languages, was only adopted as a non-binding recommendation following the UK's claim that this was beyond the competence of the Community.) Essentially the Community schemes aim to assist and encourage:

- Teacher training, and an exchange of information through the Eurydice network;
- Foreign language teaching;
- Equality of opportunity for migrant children;
- Introduction of IT in schools;

- Cooperation between universities and industry in training for new technologies (Comett);
- Student mobility, inter-university cooperation and recognition of diplomas (Erasmus);
- Exchanges for young workers (YES for Europe).

Comett

Comett is the Community in Education and Training for Technology, and aims to provide a link, at a European level, between further education and industry, with a view to addressing severe skill shortages in the new technology industries and functions. A shortage of suitably trained and qualified engineers, technicians, and programmers (let alone IT competent managers), is regrettably, not just a UK phenomenon. In the UK, however, this has been shown to be more of a restriction on growth than a shortage of capital. Whilst education-industry links have been very successful in the UK, especially in the 'science-parks', this has had only a peripheral effect on training itself. Comett has several aims, but most importantly for British industry to improve the initial training of students and continued training of skilled workers.

Designed to allow both Europe-wide programmes with their advantages of economies of scale, the programme also aims to be able to respond to local and regional needs. Essentially the activities that make up Comett are:

1 A network of education-industry partnerships;
2 Financing of student placements in industry (in member states other than their own);
3 Grants to encourage exchanges between universities and industry;
4 Cross-border continuous training projects;
5 Development of train-the-trainer packages aimed at SMEs;
6 An exchange of information and experience.

Erasmus

Erasmus, the European Action Scheme for the Mobility of Students, is a much more controversial measure potentially involving more than 6 million students in 3,600 higher education establishments. The Commission actually took the Council of Ministers to the European Court of Justice over the legal basis in 1989. While the case itself is of only passing interest, it did highlight an area of competence for the Community. The Commission argued that the Community can devise programmes with financial implications which are based on vocational training (Article 128). The UK however argued that the university education was not, as a whole, vocational because it included history, philosophy, languages, literature, politics and mathematics. While this may seem peripheral it is interesting to note what is considered by the ECJ to be vocational.

Erasmus provides a mechanism, and funding for inter-university exchanges, the output of which is education students with a full European outlook, and a better understanding, not only of the language of another member state but also its culture, economy and society – ingredients of a skilled workforce which are much sought after following 1992. The Commission's stated aim for Erasmus is to encourage future decision-makers in industry to see cross-border collaboration and joint ventures as natural and positive courses of action, rather than high-risk activities.

YES for Europe

YES is a wider ranging Youth Exchange Scheme which goes beyond the bounds of higher education, and was only agreed to in 1988. Less vocationally oriented, YES falls squarely within the theme of a 'People's Europe'. The broad purpose of the programme is to prepare young people for working life in a Community free of obstacles to the movement of people, and tries to overcome young people's resistance to moving away from their own locality. As such it had to be adopted by a unanimous vote at the Council of Ministers. YES's three year programme has a budget of 30 million ecus and anticipates supporting exchanges of at least one week, for 80,000 young people aged between fifteen and twenty-five. It is open to all young people, whether or not in education or work. As well as providing financial assistance, exchanges organized under the YES programme should ease any legal and administrative barriers involved, and provide relevant documentation and information to those non-governmental agencies organizing exchanges.

Languages

Including Gaelic and the Luxembourg language there are eleven national languages spoken (as well as several dialects such as Cornish and Catalan) within the Community. Whilst English is recognized as the language of international commerce, it is important to realize that it is not the only one. German is the most commonly spoken language of the nine in the Community, followed by English, French and Italian. Dealing with only that small percentage of the Community's businessmen and consumers who speak English will severely restrict markets and opportunities. Even in dealing with those who do understand English, a reliance on their skills and knowledge will seriously blunt any competitive edge you may have.

It is clear that the UK is in both the enviable position of having

Table 16.4   % Adults speaking European languages in Europe

Language	B	DK	F	FDR	IRE	I	N	SP	UK
English	26	51	26	43	99	13	50	13	100
French	71	5	100	18	12	27	16	15	16
German	22	48	11	100	2	6	61	3	9
Italian	4	1	8	3	1	100	2	4	2
Spanish	3	1	13	1	1	5	2	100	3
Dutch	68	1	1	3	0	0	100	0	1

Source: Gallup Survey (1986).

the most widely understood language, but the desultory position of understanding the least. It is estimated that 82 per cent of UK directors do not speak a second language, and yet the ability to communicate in a foreign tongue is not just courteous, but must make good business sense. A comprehension of a customer's language is fundamental to understanding the thinking and culture of that customer, it shows a commitment to that market, and can only help in business.

Companies expecting to engage in the wider single market, whether at home or overseas, should prepare a corporate language policy. Such a policy could be part of a European strategy, marketing/ customer service strategy, or education and training strategy, or it could even be seen as an important strategy in its own right, warranting investment (not cost). This will involve an immediate language audit which analyses use and need, along with the available skills and knowledge which will need to cover three areas:

Use – Where do we need a foreign language? (A more practical approach would be to answer the question: 'Where do we use language?') Technical writing, documentation, product labelling (important for safety requirements as well as for marketing); publications; knowledge of foreign regulations; negotiations; selling; contracting; contacting; social etc.

Also for consideration under this heading is which languages will be necessary. It may not be enough to develop corporate competence only in the languages for those countries where you want to do business. What about those continental Europeans who want to do collaborative business with you in the UK?

An eye to the wider global market is also important. Whilst Italian and German are key languages in the EC, Spanish and Portuguese are much more widely spoken languages worldwide.

Method – How should we approach the question of foreign languages, and to what degree? Drafting, translating, interpreting, conversing, printing (does your company's word-processing system have the ability to print the full range of the different European alphabets, including accents?), and culture. Different language difficulties, such as advertising copywriting, can (and probably should) be contracted-out to language professionals, but much can be achieved in-house: it may not always be advisable to use local interpreters when negotiating abroad.

Personnel – Who needs to know foreign languages? Switchboard operators (important!), receptionists, secretaries, directors, sales and marketing personnel, buyers, service departments; accounts etc.

Various options are available for improving language skills and competence. Choosing the right one will depend on the existing competence of the individuals, the use they will make of the language, and the usual criteria for training evaluation of cost and convenience. For someone who will simply need to speak in a foreign language a fairly low investment can be made for a relatively high return. It has been estimated that for most European languages just 700 words are used 70 per cent of the time in speech. However, where there is a requirement for accurate writing a deeper learning situation will be necessary.

Distance learning

Language learning is particularly well suited to distance learning techniques and a wide range of material including books, videos and audio-tapes, as well as television and radio are available. Such materials can, of course, be used many times for a number of employees. Distance learning gives flexibility in the time taken to learn, and can be used at a time of 'crisis' for immediate remedial work for those whose language use is rusty. A relatively new development in this area, for those especially interested in the spoken word is the option to learn a language by telephone. Twenty minute lessons can be given down the 'phone at regular intervals at a time which suits the learner. (This is especially useful for those who anticipate doing business by telephone where they do not have the benefit of facial expressions and sign language.)

A number of European radio stations can be received in the UK, simply listening to this regularly will do much to maintain and improve an individual's competence. As well as giving vital market and cultural intelligence, provision of foreign newspapers will also help to keep people fit for a foreign language, with the added benefit of fostering a 'European culture' to an organization.

Language schools

Language schools, although relatively expensive, offer a range of tailor-made courses, and are ideal for rapidly learning a language from scratch. Private schools can design courses of varying duration, one-on-one or in a group, residential or in-company, and tailored to the particular business need. There are a great many providers of private language training in the UK, and organizations such as the Institute of Linguists or the London Chamber of Commerce's Language Advisory & Referral Service can make recommendations on the suitability of particular trainers.

The most expensive option is for individuals to spend time at a language school abroad. Complete immersion in the culture and language of the country is, however, probably the most effective way of ensuring a sound grounding in a language.

A useful starting point for organizations is the local LX Centre. This is an initiative bringing together local further and higher education establishments with private colleges, who can provide tailored training, translation and interpreting services, and cultural briefings.

17 Marketing

With all the focus on the development of the European Community, the European Economic Area, deepening, widening and enlarging, as well as new areas of policy such as economic and monetary union, a citizen's Europe, and even common defence and security policies, it is easy to forget that the essence of the European Community is a common market. Although the term has gone out of fashion, it remains the core of the EC. The marketing management function is similarly important, and the one probably most significantly affected. This is not to say that it is the most important management function – although that could be argued – but it is the one which starts at the customer interface, and works its way through the whole operation of an organization, with an impact on research and development, design, production, distribution, customer care, finance, corporate structures and liability, human resources, use of technologies, and location. Like the quality, human resource, and indeed European and environmental functions, marketing should not be the responsibility of a single person or department, but one that runs through an organization, aware of opportunities as well as compliance requirements. This is not to suggest that there is no need for a clear marketing strategy which takes into account the changing environment presented by the single market. Indeed it should form one of the main pillars of the corporate strategy, whether or not expansion into new markets is anticipated. As ever, even if your organization is not planning to operate on a European basis, your competitors and suppliers will be.

The expanding code of single market legislation offers a number of marketing opportunities which hitherto have been impractical, or commercially unviable. It also presents a clear regime for compliance – mainly in the areas of consumer protection, but also a simplification, and easing of procedures thanks to harmonization of regulations.

The most impinging regulations are those relating to consumer and environmental protection. Most of these have been noted in previous chapters, but there are important marketing considerations which need to be borne in mind. The directive on price indications, for example, requiring goods sold in bulk to have their prices clearly displayed, allowing comparison by consumers will add a further competitive element to consumer goods marketing, putting more significance on image and branding, as well as quality. While monetary union and a single currency may seem a distant prospect, increasingly sophisticated and well-travelled consumers will be better able to make price comparisons between goods they see being marketed in different member states. If pricing is a notable selling point for a good or service, then very careful attention needs to be given to how this will be affected by greater transparency in the face of a more discriminating customer.

Economic convergence and the European exchange rate mechanism will similarly make price discrimination between member states less easy. There is, however, no absolute requirement for all goods to be sold at the same price throughout the Community, although there are restrictions, under competition law, from imposing mini-mum resale prices and preventing agents or distributors in one member state from buying or selling in another. Economic con-vergence and the progress towards a more integrated market will inevitably increase the level of competition for business. The response must be market driven. From a purely commercial per-spective, the operation of the ERM makes price competitiveness, as a result of a favourable exchange rate, an unreliable factor. The ERM forces stability into the exchange rate system – although realign-ments can be particularly turbulent. Within the core markets of the EC convergence is already happening ahead of political agreement. Benelux economies for example, no longer diverge away from the German Mark by more than 1 per cent. In the UK exporters have long relied upon a steady devaluation of the pound to ensure price competitiveness overseas. This is an unsustainable policy in the medium-term that only leads to a gradual loss of competitiveness through reliance on the cushion of low exchange rates, rather than a focus on increasing productivity.

For the marketing manager this has important implications. No longer is price the main factor of competitiveness. Other, more important, selling points need to be demonstrated to the consumer: quality, deliverability, customization are obvious areas which warrant attention, as discerning consumers look for value rather than cheapness. No product will survive long in a competitive market if it sells purely on price.

Marketing needs to be responsive to changing fashion, trends and demographics, and many trends are easily identifiable: an ageing population, and a richer youth, for example. The British Milk Marketing Board point to the fact that demand for single portion packs of ready-to-eat gateaux and luxury tarts is growing rapidly. It is predicted that the volume of single-portion packs is set to become as great as for family take-home sizes.

One of the most important developments, which is being encour-aged by the European Commission, is the greener consumer, with a keener sense of environmental responsibility. This is by no means a uniform phenomenon across the EC. Environmental concerns vary from region to region and marketing needs to be tailored to meet this divergence. There are two particular EC measures which marketing managers can either exploit to some advantage, or will be used by competitors to damage consumer confidence in a particular product.

The eco-labelling regulation will be heavily promoted by the Commission and national authorities and is likely to succeed industry's own attempts to indicate their own products are environmentally friendly. The eco-label is a stringent regime requiring rigorous standards. A clear judgement will need to be made as to whether the eco-label is valuable in marketing a product. Is the cost incurred worth more than the loss of credibility?

Perhaps the more significant weapon is a draft directive that will allow the public access to environmental information. Consumers (and competitors) would have the right to know what processes are used, what raw materials and energy are consumed in a product's manufacture. Such transparency is already being introduced in the UK through such measures as the proposed contaminated land registers. Consumers may be fooled by some current 'green' claims, but companies exposed to such freedom of information may find their credibility damaged by enquiring consumers or competitors. One oil company which advertised diesel fuel as being environmentally sound by being lead-free, has already been criticized by the Advertising Standards Authority (diesel fuel has never had any lead in it). Companies making spurious claims to environmental responsibility could be exposed to considerable ridicule if they had to make available all information on the environmental impact of its processes. Managers therefore need to pay very careful attention to their own activities, as well as those of their competitors.

One of the clear messages for marketing strategies is the lack of a homogeneous market. Cultural and historical differences are enormous, not just between member states, but between regions. Few products will genuinely qualify for a pan-European approach. Careful segmentation of markets is the most favourable option for marketing in the single market. We have already seen how regional economic performance leaves the richest regions of the Community perhaps more than twice as rich as the poorer regions. The susceptibility of consumers in such regions to particular products, as well as their patterns of discernment will vary considerably. Poor regions, such as southern Greece will be far more open to price competitiveness, whilst richer regions will be seeking better quality, but will also have a greater spending power for more luxury items, such as spending on higher quality foodstuffs, or sports and leisure services.

A simple examination of consumer spending patterns in different member states provides ample evidence of the different challenges. Differences in patterns of consumer spending make a pan-European approach to marketing — let alone advertising, impossible. At the extremes for example, Germans drink on average 143 litres of beer a year compared to the thirty-nine drunk by the French. Germans have nearly one car between two people, whilst the Greeks have just over one between ten. The British spend around $35 a head on music, whilst the Italians only spend around $8 a year. Market research and information on particular targets will clearly be a crucial element to any strategy for breaking into new markets. It is wrong to assume that simply because a product sells well in one European market that it will sell well in another. Many schemes, such as the Export Market Research Scheme, managed by the British Chambers of Commerce, exist to provide assistance to companies looking at new markets. There are no Mr and Mrs, or Monsieur and Madame Averages.

The Sara Lee cake company which has successfully expanded into new European markets, encapsulates some of the problems: 'France is our number one export market, with Germany second.' However, 'Cheesecake and lemon meringue pie do not work in Germany, while they go down well in France.'

In a more open and competitive, albeit larger, market, the challenges are likely to be greater. Market segmentation does not simply mean different approaches to promoting the same product in different areas, but a holistic approach to the output of the organization at the point when it meets the consumer. Organizations will need to be alert to the needs of their customers (whether they are one of the 340 million consumers, or one of the 18 million businesses), at all stages of the operation. Servicing of goods, for example, is an essential part of the marketing operation, along with speed of delivery, accessibility to the product or service. Careful attention needs to be given to not just the product, but also the type of organization with which the consumer wishes to deal. A very European organization, such as Benetton, has a particular appeal to those markets inhabited by consumers with a ready identity with the European Community – France and Germany, and the Benelux, and needs to provide a very European image. On the other hand, the attachment of the European flag to a piece of advertising, or packaging, for example, will curry little favour in more nationalistic markets such as the UK and Denmark where a national or even local image is important. This has huge implications for the means of distribution – do consumers want to deal with indigenous locals, or are they more likely to be impressed by the appearance of foreigners committed to their market? Of course, national prejudices can be used to particular advantage in specific markets. In the UK, electronic goods (wherever they are made) tend to sell better if they are branded with a Japanese sounding name. Similarly lagers brewed in Burton upon Trent, sell well in British pubs when they have a German sounding name. Pandering to these prejudices is vitally important to market goods effectively throughout the Community. A brief analysis of television advertisements on UK television reveals a very high number of advertisements which rely on national stereotypes, or the impact of foreign cultures in the selling of a product, or establishment of an appropriate image or style.

Such attention to national and regional cultures is vital. Marks and Spencer have even gone to the length of labelling the same soup differently for sale in different regions of the UK. In a similar vein the British New Covent Garden Soup Company has succeeded in selling French Onion Soup in France, here largely overcoming seasonality by promoting chilled summer soups. Truly European products, backed up by homogeneous European marketing are few and far between, and tend to be global products. As has already been noted there are probably no more than 50, and even amongst these there have been notable failures due to not taking a heterogeneous approach. McDonalds has succeeded in Europe through subtly tailoring its products to meet local expectations: whilst a Big Mac is the same everywhere, a cup of coffee bought in a McDonalds in France is very different from one bought in the UK! On the other hand, the difficulties experienced by the establishment of Euro Disney in France may have a lot to do with a rejection by Europeans of an alien American culture. The opening of a branch of Marks and Spencer in Paris, which has been a great success, required an enormous investment, and for the first few years made significant losses. Important marketing lessons were painfully learned when M & S simply transplanted a medium-sized UK store into the heart of Paris. It had enormous appeal to British residents, but failed to attract a sufficiently large interest from Parisians. Employing local managers, and responding to local conditions made a considerable difference, and the store is now greatly profitable.

Responding to local commercial and cultural conditions is an imperative for successful marketing. The most obvious challenges lie in the use of language. Whilst English and French are commonly understood languages throughout the EC, consumers, suppliers, collaborators, and distributors, will want to read brochures, labels, packaging, catalogues, even annual reports, and other information in their own language. Similarly they will probably want to be able to speak to representatives of the company (sales managers, service representatives, or simply shop-floor sales assistants) in their own tongue. This presents considerable opportunities for pitfalls. It is never recommended that any translations be made by an individual into anything but their mother tongue. We have all experienced the frustrations of trying to understand badly translated manuals. They reflect poorly on an organization's commitment to that market, and are an important element in the product. Edward Macbean & Co Ltd of Cumbernauld which produces textiles and protective clothing, has spent £40,000 on producing brochures in English, Dutch, French, German and Spanish.

Branding has its own dangers. Well known examples of brand names which mean unfortunate things in another language abound: soft drinks called Pschitt and Piss are unlikely to sell well in English speaking countries. One British car had its name changed at the last minute when their Spanish representative pointed out that it meant 'crash' in Spanish. Other brand names are simply meaningless — VW Golfs are sold in most of Europe as 'Rabbits', which would not have the same connotations in the UK. Other problems arise from difficulties in pronunciation, either resulting in confusion, or simply an ability of a local consumer to ask for what he wants, as each language has its own particular vowel, diphthong and consonant sounds which foreigners find difficult.

The above raises some of the difficulties and changes to the marketing environment. It is important, however, to remember, that the single market does not mean that traditional marketing methods should be rejected. Aluminium glasshouses made by Clear Span Ltd have proven to be extremely popular in Italy, following a straight-forward advertising campaign in up-market magazines in northern Italy.

Trade fairs too, remain a popular means of selling in the single market. Another British company, Railex Systems of London, succeeded in winning the contract for large filing cabinets and files for the German equivalent of the Ordnance Survey, through an enquiry at trade fairs in Leipzig and Rostock. With such a foothold the company is now confident of winning other orders from the survey departments of each German Lander.

The marketing of particular products, such as alcohol, pharma-ceuticals or food will be subject to specific regulations which managers in those organizations should be aware of. Changes to excise duties, for example, are very likely to affect different patterns of demand between different alcoholic drinks, opening up new markets for some, but making the sale of other products more difficult.

Market segmentation has long been understood as a powerful factor in marketing success, and the development of sophisticated and highly accurate targeting of mail shots, for example, bears witness to its effectiveness. However, managers need to be aware that the EC is planning restrictions on distance selling such as mail order, telephone and fax selling, televised promotional offers, and mail-shots. New data protection proposals will require those holding mailing lists to gain the permission of the data subjects before selling the lists, or using them for a different purpose than that for which the data was collected. There would also be prohibitions on the use of computers to make intuitive decisions about the person-alities of individuals. This means, for example, that a computer could not be used to sift through a mailing list to pick out, say, people who have been burgled and then try to sell them insurance. The rigidities and cost implications of such regulations mean that managers will need to rethink the cost-effectiveness of mail-shots.

On the other hand, the Community is currently examining pro-posals for the creation of an internal market in postal services. The cost of letters sent around the Community has already enjoyed some degree of harmonization — all letters posted from one point within the Community to another destination cost the same. The Commission has put forward proposals which aim to reconcile opening up postal services to competition on the one hand, but assuring a high level of minimum service throughout the whole territory on the other. Increasingly managers can expect to see more competitive services from other postal services than the traditional PTT or post offices.

One area yet to be tackled by the Commission is the wide variety of charges for telephone calls within the Community. If a marketing strategy includes a large-scale telephone operation across the Community, very careful thought needs to be given to the location of site from which calls are going to be made. In many instances it costs twice as much to make a call one way, than it does another. Calls from Spain to Denmark, for example, cost double the price of a call from Denmark to Spain.

EC proposals on telecommunications need to be borne in mind on corporate literature, brochures, letterhead paper and so on. Common international dialling codes, for example, should be used on all media which is destined for markets overseas. The Commission has proposed that the common international dialling code throughout the EC be '00'. This is most likely to be introduced into the UK in 1994. (It is also worth bearing in mind that changes to telephone codes not only impact on company literature, but also on any IT system which automatically dials other numbers, which will need resetting.)

The range of advertising media available throughout the Community is wide, and growing with the implementation of new technologies, and will need to be carefully borne in mind. Europe-wide television broadcasting has developed significantly over recent years − far more than would be expected by a non-travelling UK resident. An increasingly polyglotal population now has the ability to watch television, or listen to radio broadcasts from a number of different countries. The establishment of satellite television offers new opportunities for pan-European advertising which need to be considered. However, it remains important for local and national susceptibilities to be borne in mind. The different media have a very different impact. Companies in the UK which, for example, rely almost entirely on advertising in Sunday newspaper magazines, will need to completely rethink their marketing strategy if they want to break into the French market. For the most part very few Frenchmen read Sunday newspapers. Cinema advertising in France, on the other hand, is recognized as being tremendously powerful. Other forms of marketing and selling, which are relatively unknown in the UK, are also fairly well developed in some parts of the Community, such as Videotex in France, through the Minitel system.

A final important point, although not necessarily a marketing one, that should not be avoided is the very real ability and need of business managers to influence the direction of the development of

Table 17.1 Advertising media spend

Country	Direct	Print	Television	Radio	Cinema	Outdoor
Belgium	66	16	2	1	15	na
Denmark	47	na	na	1	2	50
France	50	21	10	2	17	na
Greece	38	50	6	na	6	na
Ireland	43	37	12	na	8	na
Italy	41	50	4	0.5	5	na
Netherlands	45	6	1	na	4	44
Portugal	26	54	13	2	5	na
Spain	50	32	13	0.5	4.5	na
UK	61	32	2	1	4	na

Source: Gibbs P. (1990) *Doing Business in Europe*. London: Kogan Page.

the European Community, and to lobby for changes to be in their favour. The code of law being developed by the EC, from directives to regulations and standards all have an impact on the way in which individual businesses will operate in the future. Unlike most national legislatures the European institutions are generally open, non-secretive, and welcoming to business input into the drafting of legislation. As most legislation being currently drafted has to do with the establishment of the internal market, its repercussions are considerable. An example of its relative openness is the use of the *fiche d'impacte*, a note which accompanies most proposals, setting out the costs to business of implementing a particular piece of legislation. Few national governments, if any, are committed to such a discipline. While the *fiche d'impacte* system is by no means perfect, it does demonstrate a commitment to understanding the true impacts of legislation, and indeed a perception of the need to make a case for legislation before it is introduced.

Lobbying in the United Kingdom has, until recently, been something of a cautious exercise, carried out discreetly, with none of the fanfare of, say, American style politics. Nevertheless, we have already seen that the European Community is a distinctly political animal, and one that is continually changing. The scope for lobbying is therefore considerable, and not something that needs to be necessarily left to the large companies, or to business representative organizations, such as Chambers of Commerce – although they have a very clear and important role. Whether we address primary legislation – directives – or technical standards, businesses stand to gain or lose considerably from whatever form the regulation finally emerges.

One immediate challenge faced by UK businesses is the overall approach to legislation in most of Europe. To over-simplify somewhat for ease of understanding, most countries which were once governed by Napoleon now have a Napoleonic Code, that is a regime of legislation which states what *is* allowed, rather than a code, such as in the UK, which states what *is not* allowed. For this reason alone it is vital that business interests are represented at the highest levels. This was clearly demonstrated by the kerfuffle over prawn flavoured crisps. The first lesson of that incident was never to believe what you read in the newspapers about the proposals emanating from Brussels; they are rarely accurate (with the notable exceptions of *The Financial Times and The Economist*). In this particular case the Commission, seeking to harmonize national regulations on banned additives in order to free up cross-border trade in food-stuffs, drew up a list of additives currently banned in the Community. Not realizing that one particular flavouring, banned in most of the rest of the EC, was actually used in the production of prawn cocktail flavoured crisps in the UK, the additive was included on the list. Newspaper headlines portrayed the Commission's move as a direct attempt to ban the crisps. The truth of the matter was that UK crisp manufacturers had not alerted the Commission to the impact of their proposals. On learning of this, the Commission quickly amended their proposal. The case clearly underlines the need to be firstly aware of the workings of the Commission, and secondly to ensure that the Commission is made fully aware of how its proposals will impact on individual businesses. Contrary to popular opinion, the European Commission is a relatively small organization, currently employing fewer people than Brent Council, or the Scottish Office, which relies heavily on external input into its deliberations.

Technical standards are a clear area where businesses can and do have considerable influence over the establishment of European standards. For the most part, Euronorms, agreed to ensure the free movement of goods, are designed to reflect the most commonly used standard in the EC so that the least number of manufacturers have to change their processes. It is clearly vital that where a business is operating to one standard that representations are made in order that standard is adopted as the European standard. Business representation on the various standardization bodies is vital. Currently, German, British and Italian standards are the most frequently adopted, almost entirely due to the efforts put in by individual businessmen prepared to spend time sitting on committees defining the European standard. Put simply, standards should not be left to chance. Any product could be made illegal at a stroke if it does not conform to a European standard, and manufacturers should ensure that they put their case through the appropriate channels.

The Treaty on European Union, and indeed the political upheavals which have resulted on the path to ratification, have made the Commission keenly aware of their need to be responsive to popular opinion, and we can expect an even more open, and susceptible Commission in the future, as it seeks to maintain support for its own programmes through both formal and informal channels of communication with business.

The first step is to remain aware of what developments are taking place. This is generally best done through a representative organization with links to Brussels, such as a Chamber of Commerce, or some of the professional institutes and trade associations. Each type of body brings its own perspective and focus of attention which may or may not be appropriate to an organization's needs. Broadly speaking trade associations will concentrate on technical and sectoral issues such as standards; professional institutes will carefully monitor the development of directives which affect their particular profession, whilst Chambers of Commerce will monitor in varying degrees of detail, all aspects of Community activity which impact on businesses generally, particularly cross-sectoral issues applying to most businesses. Alternatively organizations can rely on the official information sources of national governments and the European Commission. These do, however, tend to be very general, or overstretched, and are increasingly becoming referral services to the other bodies mentioned above. Of particular note, however, is the network of European Information Centres across the EC. Most of these are based inside Chambers of Commerce, and have direct on-line links to the Commission's own databases. They can provide enquirers with detailed information about its activities, and some also provide a monitoring service, alerting their customers to changes as they happen. Active involvement in chambers, trade associations and professional bodies is an effective way of ensuring that organizations can stay up-to-date with developments, and exercise some influence over the representations that are being made.

Representative bodies are well equipped to make representations to the Community institutions at the appropriate time, either generally on behalf of their constituency, or even raising individual cases. Membership of such a body should be part of the European strategy of all organizations. Through their own contacts in Brussels, either direct links, or through European Associations, they can be the ears and eyes of their members. Early warning of proposals is vitally important. As with all things, it is easier to change something before it gathers a head of steam. Many organizations are directly consulted by the European Commission before a proposal is ever published, and have considerable opportunity at this stage to actually change the direction of legislation. As a proposal progresses the tactics for lobbying for change adapt to the different situations. Informal consultations are often followed by the release to representative organizations in Brussels of working documents. Finally the Commission adopts a proposal (it is usually at this stage that the newspapers begin to report a proposal), and then the politics begin as it progresses through the European Parliament, the Economic and Social Committee, the Committee of Regions, COREPER, and finally to the Council of Ministers. All these organizations are themselves susceptible to lobbying and influence, and require targeting if amendments to a proposal are sought.

At the end of the day it is the Council of Ministers which needs to be convinced of a particular point of view which brings the lobbying back to national capitals. European networks are therefore vitally important at this stage. Not only are the European institutions more inclined to listen to a particular sectoral, or regional interest than a national one, but the ability to lobby all twelve governments is increasingly an important lobbying tool, especially where qualified majority voting is concerned. In many instances it will not be enough to persuade just the UK government to oppose a proposal, but also at least one other for a block to be effective. This means mobilizing support from the business community in other member states.

Nevertheless, even smaller organizations should not shy away from making direct representations themselves. Recognizing fully that lobbying is a time consuming, and highly skilled activity, there remains scope for individual managers to ensure that their voice is heard. Contacts through representative bodies will probably remain the most effective means of lobbying, but direct contacts to Commission officials, members of the European parliament, or members of the various consultative committees will always elicit a response, and are unlikely to be ignored. Nor should lobbying be confined to attempts to influence proposals for legislation. The Commission is rightly concerned about the less than total implementation and enforcement of Community legislation and is eager to learn of instances where governments, citizens, or companies are infringing regulations. This is important, and should be used to an organization's own competitive advantage. Whilst infringement proceedings may often be slow, managers should not hesitate to notify the Commission, or the national authorities responsible for enforcement where they believe that a competitor is breaking EC laws to gain particular advantage.

Above all, however, in common with the broader strategies on marketing, it is worth remembering that the Community institutions will always look more favourably on organizations presenting a generally pro-European stance. Narrow national lobbies have not proved themselves to be particularly effective. In order to further its own political aims, the Commission has always appeared more willing to listen to interest groups whose aims are to encourage European intervention. For this reason the European associations are a powerful lobby group, but small groupings bringing together organizations from more than one member state have shown themselves to be influential. Whether lobbying for change, or simply complaining about a competitor's behaviour, bodies will always be more effective if they can do so in collaboration with another organization (perhaps even another competitor) in another member state.

18 Distribution

Stimulating freedom of movement of goods should generate an actual increase in distributive operations throughout the Community. This goes far beyond the straightforward movement of freight from manufacturer to consumer. Managers looking at their distributive needs will need to examine carefully the integration of order flows, means of communications, representatives, transport, storage, inventory, assembly, packing, warehousing, and settlement. The total retail trade sector turnover in the EC is approximately 1,100 billion ecus. Distribution is an essential part of trade up to the point of sale, and, as well as forming an essential element in the cost of production, should also be considered in a structural, and marketing context. Nevertheless, the practical elements of physical distribution management in the single market are worthy of consideration as practice varies considerably throughout the Community. The table below demonstrates the extent to which concentrations of distributive ability vary between member states in terms of the number of wholesalers to retailers.

Further analysis taking into account the territories and actual number of consumers covered by each operator shows that Germany and the UK have the most heavily concentrated distribution structure, whilst the Mediterranean countries and Ireland have the most fragmented structures. This information alone points to the futility of devising a single homogeneous distribution structure for trading across the European Community. Managers will need to adapt closely to distribution structures which are prevalent in each member state. This throws into question the sought after Europeanization of management of commerce and industry in the single market. The establishment of the single market itself is having a significant catalytic effect on distribution methods. Other trends happening simultaneously also need to be taken into account.

Changing demographics, as well as family values, with a significant ageing of the population are leading to a more disparate distribution of households throughout the Community – more smaller households, as well as changes in shopping and purchasing inclinations. This implies a need for a more penetrative distribution system with an accent on services such as home deliveries and accessibility. At the same time, however, the increased use of the motor car (more cars are bought in the EC every year than people born) points to a growth in out-of-town shopping centres.

A fairly open immigration policy in the EC has led to an increase

in targeting different ethnic groups which have considerably divergent expectations in terms of goods and types of retail outlets
(particularly in the food sector). This couples with an increasingly
well-educated and sophisticated consumer seeking more information
and better quality which allows for the growth of niche marketing,
and offers opportunities for more imaginative and flexible distribution systems. Mail order and teleshopping, for example, are key
ways of responding to the social changes which have led more
consumers (particularly women) back into work and therefore
restricted access to traditional retail outlets.

Changes in production methods to accommodate greater product
differentiation, or such developments as just-in-time delivery have
a considerable impact on distribution methods, altering not just the
nature of the relationship between manufacturers and distributors
(whether within the same company or not), but also the balance
of influence. To break into new markets in Europe, confectioners
Brossard UK developed new styles of products which needed to be
fresh, and contained no preservatives. The consequent limited shelf-
life means that very close attention had to be paid to distribution
logistics, which had been inhibiting development into more distant
parts of the European Community.

The greater understanding that all sectors of the economy are
essentially service sectors has led to a growing professionalization
of distribution. For manufacturers grasping that the greatest potential
for adding value lies at the consumer end of the production cycle
the management of distribution as the link between product and
service is increasingly vital. The ability to provide deliveries at a
time and in the manner sought by the consumer is a prime com-

Table 18.1   *Retail and wholesale establishments in the EC*

Country	Retail x 1,000	Wholesale x 1,000	Ratio
Belgium	123.1	47	2.6
Germany	382.3	114	3.4
Denmark	48.7	25	1.9
France	418.2	78	5.4
Greece	184.9	25	7.4
Ireland	33.3	2	16.7
Italy	984.1	193	5.1
Luxembourg	3.7	1	3.7
Netherlands	158.6	59	2.7
Portugal	97.5	22	4.4
Spain	540.0	49	11.0
United Kingdom	343.4	112	3.1

Source: European Commission Study No 16 (June 1991). *New Intermediaries in Trade and Distribution.*

petitive weapon. In 1984 one of the key failures identified in the performance of British exporters was that threequarters of export deliveries were made late. No matter how high quality a product may be, or price-competitive, such a distribution performance will always hamper competitiveness.

Technological developments such as automation of production as well as order processing and inventory control have had a considerable impact on distribution with the growing use of electronic data interchange (EDI), for example, with considerable consequences for new skills and organizational changes. To give some indication of the penetration of new technologies into distribution, by the end of 1990 more than 60 per cent of all food sold in the EC had been barcoded and scanned at some stage in its distribution from producer to consumer. The development of EDI is probably most advanced in the United Kingdom, but growing fast in other member states. This is a development being assisted by the early standardization of coding and classification information by the European Commission through the EDIFACT programme. Managers considering implementation of any form of IT in their distributive systems will need to be aware of and conform with EDIFACT. Further more visible development include the mushrooming of electronic point of sale payments, such as Visa and Switch debit cards, at the consumer end of the distribution chain. The application of technology to the management of distribution is a matter of competitive advantage. At one end of the chain it provides scope for cost controls and greater productivity (lower space occupancy etc.); improved supply chain management; a sharper customer focus arrived at through more detailed (and faster) analysis of product ranges and customer needs at a local level; heightened quality management through better reporting.

From a wider perspective, much note has already been made about the effects of economic clustering. This is crucial to distribution management. Industrial concentrations in most EC states are moving: the economic power of the Midlands as an industrial centre has migrated south to such clusters as the M4 corridor. Similarly in Germany the hub of industrial activity has moved from the heavy industry dominated Ruhr to the high-tech industries in the South West. In France the industrial strength has shifted northwards. The implications for distribution remain unclear, but are likely to be significant, not least because of the inadequacies of the transport infrastructure to cope with such concentrations, and heightened environmental concerns.

Liberalization of the transport sector, coupled with increasing regulation of haulage will also have an impact on management distribution decisions – particularly with regard to the extent to which companies seek to manage their own distribution or contract-out. More than 750 million tonnes of goods are moved within the Community in a year, about 60 per cent of which travels by road. Legal changes resulting from such initiatives as allowing cabotage, and harmonizing technical restrictions such as lorry axle weights should have the effect of considerably lowering transport costs. If these are to be translated into improved productivity and profitability effective distribution management is essential.

The traditional pyramid of distribution of goods (manufacturer → exporter → importer → wholesaler → retailer → consumer) should therefore be subjected to review in the light of the trends identified above. There are many consequences to be considered by managers before determining their own particular strategies for distribution in the single market.

Europeanization should lead to a reduction in the number of distribution centres around the Community, but these will become larger. Anticipated improvements in transport allow companies to distribute across the whole of the European Community from a single point. The choice of that point will be considered in Chapter 22, but it is worth noting at this stage, that distribution centres will not necessarily be near to the centre of the Community; many companies, particularly non-EC companies have established their European distribution centres in Northern Ireland.

Although distribution is likely to become more centralized at distinct parts of the chain, marketing will continue to be an eclectic and locally customized process. (Think local, act European, or act local and think European?) Management of information from the local consumer to the producer will form a vital part of the distribution chain.

The commercial imperative to assure quality at the end of the supply chain, as well as the implications of liability for faulty goods, impels managers to exercise more direct control over the distribution chain. A series of different operators inevitably means weaker links. Simplification and shortening the distribution chain is clearly essential. This does not necessarily mean managing and operating the whole of the distribution system yourself, but perhaps contracting it out to one professional operator. It is worth noting at this point that the distribution chain is less and less the subject of control and decision by the producer, and increasingly the subject of influence by powerful retailers, choosing their manufacturers rather than manufacturers choosing their outlets.

Integrated logistics are inherent in the need to cut costs, improve delivery times, and ensure quality. Containerization is an obvious early step, but specialized warehousing with custom-made tracking systems which are applicable from production to the point of sale are an essential element in many distributive systems, and need to be compatible throughout the EC. Automation of distribution logistics means that a product may not be handled by humans from the end of the production line until it is picked up by a consumer from the shelf of a retail store.

The distribution and after-sales service is an integral part of the product and should not be simply an afterthought. The extent to which individual companies should be directly managing the distribution of their products and services depends greatly on the size and maturity of the organization, as well as the scale of operations and potential markets. Nevertheless, even if an organization does not see itself as being involved in distribution, and simply confines its role to getting goods out of the factory door, it will still have to respond to the changes in distribution management which are taking place so that the product can be successfully integrated. At the very least this has implications for packaging and labelling, for example.

The options for getting goods to the consumer are varied, ranging from managing haulage fleets, through to the simple operation of a mail order system, and can be contracted out at almost any stage. The initial decision needed to be taken involves not what happens when the goods leave the production line, but where they are going to reach the consumer. In Europe there are broadly eight principal types of retail outlet each with varying forms of dominance in each member state: hypermarkets, such as Carrefour (very strong in France, Spain and Portugal); supermarkets, such as Sainsbury's increasingly diversifying out of food; discount stores, such as Lo-Cost part of the Argyll Group (well developed in Germany and Denmark); mail order, such as Great Universal Stores (particularly strong in the UK, France and Denmark); chain stores, such as Marks & Spencer (very strong in the UK and Portugal); department stores, such as John Lewis (particularly prevalent in Germany and Spain); specialized stores, such as Dixons (strong in most countries); and cash and carries, such as Metro (very strong in Germany and The Netherlands).

This segmentation of retail outlets reflects the variety of means of distribution. Larger more powerful chain stores generally manage their own distribution, and the producers' responsibility lies in transporting goods to the distribution centres in an increasingly prescribed manner. Hypermarkets, and most specialized shops which may not be part of a chain, require goods to be delivered direct to the store, usually via a wholesaler. The choice of whichever retail outlet is the most appropriate for a particular good or product is a key determinant in defining the management of the producers' involvement in distribution. The Sara Lee company, with an established market in France, sought to develop a market in Germany. It discovered that its main buyers were two major frozen food home delivery groups which have franchised outlets all over the country. In Germany, home deliveries account for nearly a quarter of all frozen food purchases. For Sara Lee this means high volume orders from just two customers, rather than the difficulties in managing its own distribution network with a difficult to transport product, with a shelf-life of only eleven days.

At one end of the scale the simplest option for accessing overseas markets is simply to sell goods to an exporter. It then becomes his responsibility to deal with the administration, marketing, and transport. Inherently simple, this does preclude significant influence on pricing, servicing, and quality, which may not be in line with the brand trying to be developed, or marketing strategy. Exporting goods directly to an importer brings the manufacturer one step closer to the customer, and, provided a cooperative relationship is developed, allows the manufacturer access to local knowledge and expertise. Linking directly to wholesalers, or distributors (such as supermarket chains) requires a higher level of sales effort, which implies either a highly mobile sales force, or local agents in different markets.

In all likelihood only the largest of operators will be in a position to develop their own distribution and retail outlet networks. The costs in up-front investment and risks of failure are both high (but may be set-off against operating profits in another member state if the company is a European company, SE). Other methods of distribution which centre around joint-venture agreements should also be considered. Agency agreements are a relatively low-cost means of market entry and provide a vehicle for market distribution. In all cases of joint ventures, managers should be cautious about compliance with EC competition rules which limit exclusive distribution agreements (see Chapter 14).

One increasingly popular means of mitigating such high costs is franchising, which has accounted for the spectacular growth of many retail and distribution outlets for both manufactured goods, and services, such as Benetton, Body Shop, Holiday Inns and McDonalds. Franchising offers producers forward control of distribution to the consumer, at the same time as influence over the retailer in terms of quality and pricing, and access to local expertise and knowledge to ensure that the same product may be appropriately marketed to meet different market conditions. In 1990 there were more than 2,150 franchisers and 107,000 franchisees in the EC, accounting for more than 4 per cent of all retail sales.[89] Franchising is particularly prevalent in France and the United Kingdom. In most circumstances, and particularly for smaller operations, general franchising is granted a block exemption from the stringent competition rules under Article 85. A similar regulation providing exemptions for licensing agreements also exists.

Whether distributing goods direct to the consumer – either using existing networks such as the postal or courier services, or developing a retail network – or using intermediaries at whichever level, managers must consider the importance of the effects on their own abilities to control and manage the process, and balance the relative consequences of a variety of factors:

- Pricing policy, essentially part of the marketing function relates directly to distribution management. To what extent does the product require a uniform price across the EC? Pricing of the same product does vary considerably from member state. Is this freedom import-

ant, or can it be left in the hands of the end distributor?
- Simple procedures. All for the removal of physical and technical barriers to trade, a company's expertise may not necessarily lie in the complexities of physical distribution management. Is it worthwhile developing the new skills and resources necessary to manage distribution yourself, or should this be contracted-out as not being a core activity. On the other hand, if there is existing in-house resource, capacity and capability, is there any potential for developing this as a new product-service available to complementary companies in need of a similar distribution network?
- Distribution costs may form a substantial element of particularly bulky, low value products. The economies of scale which are available to large concentrations of distributors may be worthwhile. In a more competitive transport market, there is considerable opportunity for reducing costs. Small high value products may not, however, benefit, and developing in-house distribution systems may be more appropriate.
- Proximity to the customer, not simply in geographic terms, is crucial in managing in the single market. If the distributions systems are removed from the production systems, or out of the control of company management, there is a danger that information flows will be so extended that the company cannot be sufficiently responsive to changing customer needs. Similarly the ability to control quality and provide services may be difficult when using intermediaries. On the other hand, it may be impossible for a small company to supply adequate local product service, in which case the distributor may be able to. Alternatively other joint venture arrangements may be necessary.

To turn briefly to actual transportation considerations, as affected by the single market: as with the wider distributive networks it is unlikely that all but the largest of organizations will find it viable or desirable to transport their own goods to market. Contracting the responsibility for transportation to specialist companies is, in most cases, not only more cost-effective, but also removes much of the hassle involved in documentation, packaging and marking, insurance, carriers' liability, and permits. Nevertheless there are several options which warrant consideration, particularly if there are special delivery implications. Many buyers will wish to manage their own transportation requirements, but others will be wary of the hidden costs involved, or even the foreign exchange implications. Increasingly when tendering for contracts, tenders are made including delivery. As an island, companies in the UK have particular transport needs in crossing the Channel, which have led to the dominance in the freight transport market of the road trailer, which is well suited to ferries, and is more than competitive with air freight.

Air freight benefits from rapid movement between airports, but suffers considerably from the times involved at either end, which mean that, at least for the golden triangle markets, air freight is unlikely to be any quicker than road. Of course in the case of special deliveries, which travel accompanied, air freight will usually continue to prevail as the most efficient means. Increasing competition between European airlines may have the effect of stimulating the introduction of new services to exporters and importers along the lines of Red Star Parcels, where collection and delivery is carried out by the transporter. This is currently a service being carried out by express transporters, such as DHL, dealing in smaller consignments which need rapid guaranteed delivery.

The potential of rail freight has been largely neglected in Europe, and particularly in Britain with its poor record of unreliability over long periods of time. Usage of rail has been largely confined to bulk goods, such as coal or aggregate, which are too heavy to be carried by road. However, both the European Commission's own push to encourage the development of railways for environmental reasons, and the opening of the Channel Tunnel will vastly increase the opportunities for rail freight. Again, like air transport there are modal difficulties in door-to-door deliveries, but in many parts of the EC, particularly in Germany, the rail network remains dense, and private sidings relatively common amongst the larger economic operators. It is estimated that the Channel Tunnel will only be able to accommodate 6 per cent of the current cross-Channel freight movements. Nevertheless its introduction will allow the development of rapid rail links between the major cities of Europe and Channel Tunnel high speed trains will certainly be a suitable vehicle for express deliveries of smaller packages.

There are a number of legal aspects to distribution which need to be taken into account, in addition to the commercial and managerial considerations above. In line with the abolition of customs duties no member state is allowed to charge a duty for administrative services at borders; for unloading; for storage on products deposited in public warehouses during completion of customs formalities; processing of imported goods simply because they have crossed a border. Of particular relevance to UK exporters and importers however, is the continued existence of shipping light dues − a tax on ships docking in British ports to cover the costs of navigational aids, which is not levied in any other member states, and adds considerably to some shipping costs. This may make Rotterdam a cheaper 'hub' for imports and exports on a Europe-wide basis, than any of the UK ports.

For the removal of barriers to trade there remains a certain amount of paperwork which affects distribution of goods around the Community. The new VAT regime has already been examined. The thrust is for a progressive abolition of documentation at borders, including the single administrative document used for customs clearance procedures, nevertheless it remains likely that some forms of documentation will still be required for the movement of most goods across the Community. This remains a complex area, and the employment of specialists, such as freight forwarders, is recommended if unnecessary and costly delays are to be avoided, whether goods are being moved by haulage or by post. A community Carnet can be used for the temporary exportation of goods for sale of exhibition purposes. Certain goods, particularly those relating to food, agriculture, veterinary or phytosanitary controls may also be subject to end use, destination or exportation formalities.

19 Innovation

One of the integral themes, in the responses of the marketing and production functions to the challenges of the single market, has been the need for product differentiation and segmentation as a means to retaining competitiveness. The wider range of suppliers responding to more sophisticated and discerning consumers are able to provide products which are better suited to the precise individual needs of the customer. As consumers, everywhere we look we have more choice. Gone are the days when a supermarket would simply sell potatoes, now most outlets are selling more than ten different varieties for different flavours, and different types of cooking. The same is true for nearly every single product and service on the market. Why should consumers any longer buy a product which does not exactly match their needs? Exactly the right shade of blue, in a paint colour; exactly the right size of cupboard in the kitchen; exactly the right specification of computer — no more and no less.

Innovation is a driving force behind product differentiation, but is necessary, and cannot be ignored for a number of reasons. Most importantly compliance, cost efficiency, and competitive edge. Ignoring innovation, companies increase the risks of obsolescence, out-moded and inefficient production, and at worst their products being banned for failure to meet environmental, consumer protection, or health and safety standards, on top of consumers not wanting to buy their products.

From the Community perspective it is clear that Europe has lost its competitive edge compared to the US and Japan with regard to future technology. Research by the US Department of Commerce shows that European industry is ahead of US innovators in digital imaging, and flexible manufacturing systems, but is level or behind in advanced semi-conductors, high-density data storage, sensor technology, superconductors, advanced materials (such as ceramics and polymers), artificial intelligence, high performance mathematical co-processors, biotechnology, electronic optical equipment (such as fibre-optics) and medical equipment. These are all areas which are likely to be crucial in competitiveness of products or processing in the coming years.

Research and development spending in the EC overall compares fairly favourably with global competitors, to the extent that there are a number of industry specializations where European industries are leading. German companies are extremely strong in mechanical engineering and cars; Italian industry has developed particular expertise in finished chemicals and textiles; the UK is strong in the defence sector; whilst Dutch companies have developed and maintained a specialization in electrical and electronic technologies – here we clearly see economic clustering as a phenomenon. The problems lie not so much in the quantity, or even quality of research and development in the EC, but in the inability of firms to integrate R & D and innovation in an overall strategy which succeeds in bringing new products to market. It has become abundantly clear that the failure lies in a bifurcation between innovators and marketeers. There is a serious gap between innovation and efficient production – an even wider gap exists between research and actually responding to the needs and aspirations of consumers.

Twentieth-century technology and manufacturing processes, heavily reliant on mass production and standardization have to give way to flexibility which can combine economies of scale with the scope for variety. This can only be achieved by the development of new products in the context of a rapid and continuous programme of innovation which preempts the shorter product life-cycle.[89] Having identified the problem, the Community's involvement in innovation is not a clear cut one. As the Commission notes:

> Responsibility and initiative must lie in the first instance with firms themselves. Action undertaken by the public authorities and by firms must stay within the four corners of the Community's international commitments, the rules governing the operation of the single market, and the rules of competition. Otherwise one man's gain will be another's loss and there will be no all-round increase in industrial competitiveness.[90]

The Community's involvement in the question of innovation is therefore restricted to providing the appropriate framework for stimulating research and technological development, i.e. an effective code of intellectual property and European technical standards, and harnessed by the need to deal only with pre-competitive research. At the same time the focus of attention is on encouraging cross-border collaboration. Nevertheless the current third Programme for Research and Technological Development has a budget of 5.7 billion ecus, which is not an insignificant sum, and represents an important resource which is available to companies operating within the EC's goals, and not just the largest of companies.

The point about Europe-wide policies for innovation is inherently a single market point, and one which should reflect directly on company thinking: as research costs escalate, with the potential for payback being limited by shorter product-cycles, businesses must make the most of the opportunities offered by the size of the wider common market. There are six separate areas of Community innovation activity which impact on most areas of commerce and industry:

1   Enabling technologies
   - Information technologies
   - Communications technologies
   - Development of telematics
2   Industrial technologies
   - Industrial and materials technologies
   - Measurement and testing
3   Management of natural resources
   - Environment
   - Marine sciences and technologies
4   Life sciences and technologies
   - Biotechnology
   - Agricultural and agri-industrial research
   - Biomedical and health research
   - Life sciences and technologies for developing countries
5   Energy
   - Non-nuclear energies
   - Nuclear fission safety
   - Controlled nuclear fusion
6   Optimization of intellectual resources
   - Human capital and mobility

The development of innovation policy lies largely with the Committee on Scientific and Technological Research (CREST), made up of representatives of member states, which has a responsibility to coordinate national policies and develop the programmes.

Cooperation between competitors on pre-competitive research is not a simple thing for companies to contemplate or manage, but is a vital strategic weapon to achieving global competitiveness. The basic paradox of sharing information and resources with direct competitors is an important one. A clear understanding of the purpose of the collaboration project is important, along with an agreement of where pre-competitive research starts and stops. Nevertheless opportunities exist and should be sought out. This could range from developing new materials or processes in order to achieve compliance with new regulations, through to sharing the by-products of other research programmes.

The largest of the EC programmes is the ESPRIT programme (European Strategic Programme for Research in Information Technologies), whereby the Community provides half-funding for research projects where there is collaboration between companies or academic or scientific bodies from more than one member state. The Commission has gone to great lengths to ensure the involvement of SMEs, for example, by introducing a system of blind tenders, so that the advisory board (made up of the twelve largest European companies[91]) does not know where the bid is coming from. Looking at the list above, it is important for smaller companies not to feel that there is little of relevance here. Certainly the 'big science' areas, such as nuclear fission will have little direct impact, but the programmes on developing environmentally friendly technologies, for example, or new industrial materials will be directly beneficial. Calls for proposals are widely disseminated, and companies should keep in touch through the EC's information apparatus such as the local European Information Centres, BC-Net, Euro-Net Diane, or the *Official Journal*.

One of the most effective means of EC involvement in innovation is through ensuring community-wide programmes of technology transfer. Most basic research is done in the public sector, in universities and hospitals for example, which often does not find its way into the hands of the private sector, and is rarely developed into viable commercial products. Similarly many innovations developed, often by large companies, which may have valuable spin-offs or considerable potential, are not brought to market because they do not fall within a particular company's corporate strategy. It is therefore important that these opportunities are maximized throughout the EC, and duplication of research and waste of resource is minimized.

For smaller companies which do not have the capacity or resource to put considerable weight into research and technological development programmes, the opportunities presented by both collaboration of pre-competitive research, as well as technology transfer are most important. In the latter case there are numerous national and even local programmes, such as the development of science parks which bring together local industries with academia and the peripheral support services, benefiting all those involved, by bringing together scientific expertise, with commercial experience.

Of particular relevance is the SPRINT (Strategic Programme for Innovation and Technology Transfer) programme which is aimed principally at small and medium sized enterprises. SPRINT provides funding to local business support organizations such as chambers of commerce, development and enterprise agencies, and innovation centres to diffuse technological advances. More and more of these organizations are now in a position to provide direct assistance to companies seeking partners for innovation.

It is something of a truism in the UK, that we are not short of inventions, merely deficient in innovation. The distinction is a significant one. Innovation means bringing invention to market. One of the greatest obstacles and deterrents to innovation, apart from the cost, is the risk of not being able to recoup the costs of the initial research and development. The notion of intellectual property is to protect the innovator from competition for long enough to recoup those costs. If there were no protection then competitors would swiftly steal the results of research and reap the benefits. The code of law which has developed around intellectual property is a complex one involving copyright, trademarks and patents, and has largely come about outside the remit of the European Community through such mechanisms as the Luxembourg Convention on Patents, and the Berne Convention on Copyright. Not only have these instruments failed to achieve a coherent level of protection, but they have also failed to keep up with technological developments, unable to provide clear protection for such developments as computer software or biotechnology. The European Community began its work on intellectual property in 1959, and progress has been slow.

Two significant problems face managers in the European context who need to protect their intellectual property. Firstly, the lack of adequate protection around the world. Counterfeiting and copying, a fact of life, particularly in the Far East, is something being addressed in the Uruguay Round of the GATT Treaty. Secondly the difficulties involved in registering patents, for example, in twelve different countries. Differences in intellectual property laws not only inhibit innovation, but also intra-Community trade. Lord Cockfield, in his original Internal Market White Paper, identified the urgent need for agreement over a European Community Trademark, which would enable innovators to apply for a single trademark protecting their invention throughout the EC.

The Luxembourg Convention on Patents established the European Patents Office in Munich, but to date has merely simplified the process of applying for national patents – considerable difficulties still remain, not least with presenting a patent in the appropriate languages of the Community. The development of the Community Patent Convention is aimed at a common system of law which will be implemented by individual member states, but has yet to be ratified by all twelve countries, and so has not come into force.

The EC is moving towards a European trademark system which would provide genuine protection throughout the Community, without the need to register a trademark in all member states. This would considerably ease the burden of obtaining protection. Argument continues at the Council of Ministers on the site of the European Trademark Office, and the working language, nevertheless there is a commitment to the system in principle, which is set out in a regulation which defines the criteria for registration, the validity of the Community trademark, and the procedures for acquiring it.

20 Information and communications technology

The establishment of the wider single European market reaches into all areas of business. One of the responses common to most functions of management is the greater and enhanced use of information technology (IT). It is a growing fact of life, from the PCs on nearly all managers' desks, to the improving services, ease of use, and lower costs, which are transforming the way Europe does its business. As a catalyst of change the creation of the single market is only outstripped by the development of new technologies, particularly information technologies. It is salutary to think that ten years ago the facsimile machine was a novelty in most organizations. Now more than half of all transatlantic telephony is non-voice traffic:[92] fax, electronic data interchange (EDI), and computers interrogating each other. The three core technologies which are changing commerce and industry (physical technology – bar codes etc. and imaging techniques; communications technology – fax, and modems etc; and information processing technologies) are advancing at an astonishing rate, and have benefited in the EC from considerable support from the European Commission through both the research programmes, and the legislative frameworks, particularly the development of standards.

The speed of development cannot be underestimated, nor its potential for revolutionary change in any organization underrated. To take possibly the most extreme example of visionary adaptation to new technologies, the People's Republic of China covering one of the largest territories in the world and with the largest population, faced with the challenge of improving telephonic communications is implementing a great leap forward by ignoring the development of land-based technologies and moving directly to cellular digital satellite networks. Planting one satellite in geostationary orbit above China, and issuing anyone who wants one with a portable telephone removes at a stroke the need for millions of miles of cabling, and brings what was a relatively backward nation straight into the twenty-first century. All companies can achieve similar (if not on such a scale) leaps; not just halving costs, or doubling or trebling their productivity or capacity, but increasing it a hundred- or a thousand-fold by the effective implementation of new information technologies. There have certainly been (expensive) disappointments with the introduction of IT into organizations, but in a single market which covers a wide territory, and an enormous population, where

competitive advantage is essentially efficient, distributive and differential by nature, IT provides the vehicle to gain not simply an
edge, but a march over competitors.

An efficient marketplace relies on information being transmitted
rapidly — it is the function of the market to place a value on that
information, and commerce and industry to react to it. IT offers
organizations the opportunity to gain immediate access to the
information requirements relating to supplies, production, and most
importantly to consumer demands, rapidly and accurately.

Nearly 7,000 supermarkets in the UK — more in France — are now
equipped with the necessary technology to take information about
sales directly from the check-outs back through the whole of the
distribution chain to the suppliers (and in some cases) their suppliers
in an instant, allowing not just an immediate replacement of the
good sold, but accurate and critical marketing information to be
made available and acted upon within hours instead of weeks. It is
thus an essential element to product differentiation, the response of
quality, and added-value services.

The distributive impacts are two-fold: not only does IT allow
different corporate structures and hierarchies, but more directly
newer management techniques, such as just-in-time to come to the
fore. In the UK, it takes just forty-two minutes from ordering carpets
for the Nissan Primera car from the nearby factory to them being
made, delivered and fitted into the new car,[93] which is destined for
the European markets. This is something that goes far beyond
simple cost minimization. Information technology allows the establishment and development of the European network organization,
which links together the interests of the core activities of an organization, its suppliers, distributors, the peripheral service activities,
its customers, collaborators and shareholders in a manner which
transcends national boundaries. This is important not simply in
terms of efficiency, but also, as has been noted, in the ability to
deliver quality throughout the distribution chain — important not
only as a competitive edge, but also with regards to compliance
with consumer protection legislation. Tying in the supplier to the
manufacturer to the distributor ensures effective control on quality,
pricing and marketing. The consequences for all those involved in
that chain are immediate. Whether an organization is at the raw
material supply end of the chain, or interfaces directly with the
retail consumer, they will increasingly find themselves part of an
elaborate and sophisticated information technology network which
will exercise growing and direct control over the processes and
operations which supply the next or previous step in the chain.

Again, this is not simply something just for the large company,
but an appropriate response by even the smallest of organizations
seeking to extend their market penetration throughout the EC. The
distribution of information around the network organization is much
more than simple office automation. One retail financial services

firm has transformed itself from being able to answer 90 per cent of clients' queries within fourteen days, to 90 per cent within ten minutes.[94]

One of the clearer ways in which IT can be exploited to competitive advantage in the single market is a further aspect to the distributive factors: the distribution of work. One of the paradoxes about the concentrative effects of economic clustering is that it does not necessarily imply that the whole of one organization's functions need to be in one place. It is clusters of functions that will matter, and many of those clusters will be geographically apart from others thanks to the potential of information technologies. Most office-based functions can be away from the manufacturing or distribution sites; either distributed and dispersed, or centrally located on the periphery of the Community and therefore benefiting from such aspects as cheaper labour. By way of example, Colin and Susan Coulson Thomas, acknowledged experts and practitioners in their field, have identified a number of tasks suitable for tele-commuting:[95] computer programming, data entry, form processing, book-keeping and accountancy, invoicing, estimating, planning, report preparation, research analysis, graphic design, and word-processing. Issues relating to location of functions will be examined in the final chapter, but the ability to link functions with functions and with customers, suppliers and distributors across long distances should not be lost on managers planning their European IT strategies.

The European Community's interventions in the realm of information technology have a direct impact on the distributive consequences on the management function. With the push towards the establishment of trans-European networks there is an especial attention being paid to links with islands and peripheral regions of the Community. A Europe-wide commitment to open systems will encourage demand for and therefore upgrading of trans-frontier communications networks.

Establishment of the single European market in information technology will in itself have a considerable impact on business support services in the EC. The fragmentation, lack of standards, and high costs which have resulted from the lack of a coherent market are making way for integrated, open systems, which are driving down the costs of information technology. Assisted by the various EC programmes (ESPRIT, IMPACT, DIANE, ECHO, DRIVE, DELTA, AIM and DIME) coupled with the agreement of true European standards in the fields of telecommunications will allow businesses to maximize the potential offered without the significant risks which have been suffered to date. This manifests itself across the board, from the ability to use the same mobile telephone anywhere in the Community, to the possibility of EDI between suppliers and buyers in any member state through the Commission's trade electronic data interchange system (TEDIS) which brings together the relevant computers of public administration – such as customs and excise formalities, and the private sector – such as freight handlers and export agents. Looking further into the future, the adoption of an agreement on Integrated Services Digital Network (ISDN)[96] which allows combined voice and data telephony, and standards for packet-switching, opens up considerable opportunities and cost-savings in telecommunications networks. A wide range of Europe-wide IT services, designed to improve the effectiveness of European businesses can be expected to be developed within the framework of the internal market for communications.

One particular area which warrants attention for companies seeking to operate on an international basis is cross-border payments systems. Whether importing or exporting, the complications and costs of cross-border payments will remain until full monetary union has been achieved. European Cooperative banks have taken a useful initiative by establishing TIPA (Transferts Interbancaires de Paiements Automatisés) which aims to cut the high cost of low value cross-border payments. For companies selling products or services abroad for sums of less than around £50, almost all their profit will be wiped out by the exchange costs of transferring money from one country to another. TIPA is a European network which transmits live payments through the automated clearing systems of UK, French, Belgian, Germany and Italian banks, allowing direct transfers from one bank account to another at a fraction of the usual cost. At a charge of £5 for ad hoc transactions, but much less for bulk payments, the system will be of considerable value to consumers and small businesses alike.[97]

Of particular relevance to businesses amongst the Commission's own interventions in information technology are the establishment and development of particular services aimed at fostering cross-border collaboration, the Business Cooperation Network (BC-Net) and the opening up of public procurement markets, Tenders Electronic Daily (TED).

BC-Net is a computerized system aimed at encouraging SMEs to cooperate between member states, which holds a profile of thousands of companies on a database, and is able to match needs, bringing together, for example, suppliers and distributors, or potential partners in EEIGs. A completely commercially confidential service, it can be accessed through European information centres and a number of chambers of commerce, as well as certain local authorities. TED is an information service provided by the Commission which lists all appropriate opportunities for tendering for public sector contracts (see Chapter 11), which can be accessed through any organization which is a customer of ECHO, such as a European Information Centre.

There are also a number of separate databases which have been developed by the EC to assist businesses with their information needs: CALL, CELEX, COMEXT, CRONOS, DIANE GUIDE, EABS,

ELISE, ENDOC, EUROSTAT and REGIO. For organizations which do not have direct access to on-line information, the source of all information is the *Official Journal of the Community*, which contains all proposals for legislation, regulations and offers for tenders.

Within the UK the infrastructure of business information services has tended to be fragmented, suffering from in some cases duplication, but in other gaps in the services provided. Nevertheless all these organizations are in a position to provide information: European Commission; chambers of commerce; European info-centres; Department of Trade and Industry; professional institutes; trade associations; British Standards Institute; British Overseas Trade Board; Training and Enterprise Councils (TECs and LECs).

The information requirements of managers operating in the single market are considerable, ranging from advance warning of legislative changes through to detailed market information and research, export opportunities, efficient sources, openings for cooperation and collaboration, and personal contacts. Awareness of technological and research developments, as well as social, economic, cultural and political trends all add to the mass of information which managers will need to deal with in the course of operating in the single market. Clearly systems will need to be in place to cope with this kind of overload. Too much information is often worse than too little, and it is singularly appropriate for much of this work to be delegated to organizations geared up to dealing with business support bodies, such as chambers of commerce. (During 1991 British chambers of commerce dealt with a query from business every twelve seconds – far more than any other organization in the UK.) At the same time, efficient use of information technology allows information to be sorted and filtered, analysed and synthesized into manageable formats. Managers will need to be discriminating in their reading; discerning in their briefings and conferences, and selective about their access to information sources. Effective use of information technology, and the establishment of appropriate corporate structures and hierarchies which enable information to travel in both directions, as well as horizontally and vertically through an organization, unfettered by demarcations and national boundaries will provide the appropriate means of dealing with the coming information overload.

21 Finance

Financial management is clearly crucial to the success of any business. Having assessed the product, invested in the design and innovation, created a marketing plan, trained and recruited, any company remains akin to a shark: it must keep moving to stay alive, and that means cashflow – as important in the European market as in any other. Finding sources of finance, managing risk, working with the foreign exchanges, as well as dealing with other financial services such as insurance and credit guarantees will be relevant to any manager working in the single market, and effectively represents the pivot upon which the whole operation turns. Political uncertainties make the timetable towards the fulfilment of European economic and monetary union uncertain. However, in the development of the single market it has always been the case that the business community has been several steps ahead of the politicians, and managers should already be taking advantage of the freedom of movement of capital and establishment of financial service, and preparing for the ecu.

As with most functions, the effects of the development of the single market fall into the two categories of compliance, and commercial threats and opportunities. In addition there are the fiscal implications. The essence of the impact of the single market on the finance function is in line with the single market philosophy of a level playing field within a free market. The corporate demands for such activities as accounting or shareholder prospectuses, as well as the rules of the game in such areas as insider dealing are all effectively harmonized so that competitors do not have an unfair advantage. The flip side is to liberalize the financial markets to ensure a free flow of capital and financial services throughout the Community in order to stimulate competition and thus improve choice, the quality of services, and hopefully drive the cost of financial services (but not necessarily the cost of finance) down for the benefit of the commercial and industrial sectors. At the same time it allows for the development of truly pan-European financial services.

The starting point is the freedom of movement of capital services. One of the very first things Margaret Thatcher's new Conservative Government did when it came to power in 1979 was to remove all exchange controls. This anticipated a 1988 Community directive[98] which required all member states to do so. In fact, this is now the case in most member states although the more recent joiners have temporary derogations: exchange controls still exist in Greece and Portugal which may continue until 1995. Italy finally abolished its exchange controls in May 1990. Mrs Thatcher's initiative was not an innovative one. The requirement to abolish exchange controls is contained in the original Treaty of Rome (Article 67) and is fundamental to the free flow of goods and services across frontiers. This, of course, has removed a considerable obstacle to trade, not only facilitating the payment of goods, and the ability of businessmen to travel freely, but also allowing companies with overseas operations to repatriate profits. This freedom is very much taken for granted now, but any manager now doing business in a country where strict exchange controls exist will appreciate the difficulties that can be caused by seemingly petty restrictions. The directive also permits nationals or companies of other member states to open bank accounts abroad.

The next step in stimulating a free market in financial services is to allow banks and other financial institutions to open branches and operate freely in other member states. Principally for reasons of consumer protection, but also as instruments of macro-economic policy, banks have always been subject to rigid regulation as to their activities, solvency and supervision. Some degree of harmonization of supervisory regimes was therefore essential, and the Community has embarked upon a detailed programme to approximate banking laws as a precursor to allowing any bank established in one member state to operate freely in another.

The first and second banking directives have established a regime which caters for a basic right of establishment throughout the EC, and the conditions under which a banking licence may be granted or withdrawn. This covers a wide range of activities which impact on business managers: current accounts, deposit taking, fund management, leasing agreements, lending, securities, money transmission and underwriting, and applies to all forms of 'banks' including cooperatives and building societies. The second directive requires all banks to have a minimum capital base of 5 billion ecus.

The advantages to business from a liberalized banking system are numerous. The extension of the range of international banking services which may be offered by a company's own bank will greatly simplify administrative procedures relating to trade. The ability to use the services of a foreign bank also gives business access to direct knowledge, expertise and advice about a local market. If a business is seeking to expand its operations in another member state, the active assistance of a local bank will be invaluable, whether this be the Madrid branch of Barclays, or the Manchester branch of Crédit Lyonnais. Increased competition between banks should also stimulate better levels of service. Initially this is only likely to be felt by larger customers, but increasingly foreign banks in the UK are targeting smaller enterprises.

The ability to 'shop around' the EC for financial services immediately raises the possibility of new sources of funding. For most small and medium sized organizations the principal source of

Table 21.1 Liberalization of financial services

Financial services directives

- 1st and 2nd banking coordination
- Solvency ratios
- Insider trading
- Money laundering
- Harmonization of investment services
- Capital adequacy
- Capital movements

funding is debt, in the form of secured loans or overdrafts. The development of the European Exchange Rate Mechanism, which reduces volatility in exchange rates, takes a good deal (but by no means all) of the risk out of foreign currency loans. This still remains a clear matter of judgement for businesses, but it may be the case that if low interest rates are being offered in one member state then that may be the appropriate place to seek finance. Caution needs to be exercised however. The events of September 1992 highlight the real dangers of devaluation. A company which had taken a loan in German Marks would have found itself paying 10 per cent more in effective interest payments overnight as a result of the devaluation of sterling. The development of foreign currency loans has grown considerably in both the corporate and consumer sectors (mortgages for example).

The development of the European Exchange Rate Mechanism has certainly been effective in containing day-to-day exchange rate flexibility, but even within the system, the fluctuations possible are not inconsiderable and can seriously erode profit margins. One way in which the risks of exchange rate volatility can be minimized is to take out loans denominated in ecus, which, as a basket of currencies, is the least erratic unit of exchange. Moves towards economic convergence will have a considerable impact, not just on Treasury operations, but need to be carefully considered in the context of all overseas financial operations. Until monetary union, with its single currency, is established, finance managers will be able to take advantage of the wide range of ecu-denominated instruments to minimize the down-size of risk, as well as reinforcing their own commitment to Europeanization, by pricing contracts in ecus which benefits not only the supplier but also the buyer.

A controversial draft directive[99] on harmonization of laws regarding investment services will, when adopted, widen further the range of financial services which will benefit from an open competitive market. Broadly the directive will allow an investment company (any firm which engages in securities-related transactions) which is licensed to operate in its home country to establish operations in any other member states. The directive provides minimum levels of protection for investors by specifying the arrangements for customers' money and securities, necessary compensation schemes, as well as exchanges of information between regulators. It also opens up access to the stock markets of other member states.

There are a considerable number of measures relating to insurance which will similarly open up the markets with the intention of boosting competition and thereby raising quality standards and the range of services available, by harmonizing and liberalizing the regulation of insurance provision throughout the EC. Insurance is a quickly growing market, and managers themselves need to be fully aware of the growing areas of potential liability which Community legislation opens them up to. Environmental and consumer protection legislation in particular raise significant obligations on producers, distributors, importers and exporters which must be insurable risks. Significant Court of Justice decisions have already established the precedents that an insurance company no longer has to be based in the member state where the risk is being covered. The options for cross-frontier provision of insurance are therefore available and should be used. In an increasingly litigious age, where penalties and regimes still vary considerably from one member state to another, areas of European activity which companies should be examining their insurance cover include: industrial, commercial and professional risks, consumer protection, environmental liabilities, motor liability, libel, credit, and legal expenses.

A further point on finance and cash flow relates to credit controls and the late payment of debt. For smaller firms this has always been a major problem. Collecting debts is never easy at the best of times, and can only be made more difficult when operating across frontiers and larger distances. Credit checking will clearly be important − this is an area where local chambers of commerce can help. Furthermore there is currently a range of different regimes across the Community, including statutory interest payable on debt, and in some circumstances it is a criminal offence (rather than a civil one under contract law) to make a late payment. The European Commission has been considering, for some time, introducing EC legislation on late payment, but this has proved controversial and has yet to emerge. Although standard terms of payment contract average around sixty days, practice itself varies considerably, ranging from an average of forty-five days for payment in France, to more than ninety days in Italy.

One of the largest cost factors which managers need to bear in mind in their financial planning is the liability for different forms of corporation tax. Company taxation is an extremely complex arena in the context of the single market. National fiscal regimes have taken decades to develop, and as a result of expedient change and government intervention tend to be sophisticated to a level of incoherence. Taxation of companies in modern economies serve two real functions: firstly to raise revenue to fund public expenditure, and secondly to influence corporate behaviour by penalizing some activities, but providing beneficial arrangements for others. The evolution of a truly harmonized regime for European corporation tax remains therefore a distant prospect – although one that remains firmly in the goals of the European Commission.

The Community's main activities on corporation tax are driven by the need to eliminate as much as possible, distortions to competition. The Community has therefore concentrated so far on trying to resolve those issues of taxation which are inhibiting cross-frontier activities. The next stage would be to establish common systems, and then common tax rates. Unsurprisingly this is an area of significant political controversy, and most of the proposals have yet to be agreed. Nevertheless managers will need to take careful account of the fiscal implications of their activities in order to minimize, and in some cases, avoid liability. A 1975 proposal to harmonize corporation tax rates has now been withdrawn as a result of an inability to reach agreement. (Fiscal affairs directives, can only be adopted by the Council of Ministers by unanimous agreement.) A recent study, the Ruding Report, however, has resuscitated the aim of harmonized rates, by demonstrating the clear distortions to competition that arise. With agreement now reached on minimum levels of indirect taxation (VAT and excise duties), differences in direct taxation no longer balanced by variations in indirect taxation, constitute real obstacles to fair competition. The UK, for example, currently enjoys the lowest rate of corporation tax, for smaller companies, of any other member states.

The principal measures are:

- A Directive on the common system of taxation of mergers, divisions and transfers of assets, and exchange of shares of companies in different member states (EEC/90/424)
- A directive on arbitration procedures designed to eliminate double taxation of profits transferred across borders (EEC/90/436)
- A proposal that member states allow losses incurred by a branch or subsidiary to be set off against the tax liability on the profits of the parent at home (COM(90)595)
- A proposal covering tax treatment of carry-over losses (COM(85)319)
- A proposal for harmonizing withholding taxes on the repatriation of dividends (COM(90/435)

The proposal to allow tax losses of a branch or subsidiary in one member state to be set off against profits in another is probably the most important, but regrettably the least likely to be adopted. In the meantime there is a crucial need for managers to be keenly aware of the fiscal implications of their EC activities. Corporation tax rates vary significantly from country to country, along with exemptions and reliefs. There are, of course, ways and means of transferring profit and loss across borders — such as raising service charges on subsidiaries, for example — to ensure that the tax treatment of multinational affairs is favourable.

22 Purchasing

It is a fundamental tenet of the single market that the stimulation of competition will drive down prices and improve quality. All those aspects covered so far with regard to segmentation, market responsiveness, customer discrimination and discernment, and deliverables operate to the benefit of the purchaser. Furthermore, the process of economic convergence and integration is by its very nature a deflationary one. Of course, this may present problems to governments seeking to stimulate their economies, but deflation remains a boon to purchasers (provided supply remains economically feasible, and demand sufficiently strong to prompt real competition between suppliers). Essentially the purchasing function will enjoy a wider choice of suppliers, goods and services, at a lower price, all the way through the supply chain, and across all operations.

There are no businesses or individuals who are not consumers or purchasers of one kind or another, whether this be raw materials, business support services, energy, transport, communications, travel or simple consumables such as stationery. Managers must therefore take advantage of the opportunities being offered in the purchasing field as a result of the completion of the single market. It should not be necessary to rehearse all those areas in which Community level interventions will benefit purchasers in terms of more competition, new sources of supply and lower prices resulting from the free movement of goods, the removal of non-tariff barriers and the minimization of costly bureaucracy. There are, however, a number of particular areas which warrant attention by purchasing managers.

The purchasing of goods and services by organizations happens at nearly all the operational levels in the supply chain up to the customer. This may take the form of raw materials or components at the beginning of a manufacturing process, packaging towards the end of the production process, or the means of transport to get the goods to the market. It can also include the purchasing or subcontracting of service contracts, marketing expertise and consultancy, professional advice, or print buying. At all stages purchasers will need to pay particular attention not just to the benefits of cost reduction, but also to the pressures of quality control in a competitive environment. The end-user's perception of the quality of a particular good or service will be highly dependent on the quality of inputs into that good or service. The weakest link in the supply chain will determine the quality to the customer.

Of perhaps greater importance are the implications for consumer and environmental protection. Product and service liability for defective or dangerous goods is joint and several, and a manufacturer will find himself equally liable to the consumer for the failure of a defective, externally sourced component as the manufacturer of that component. Purchasers will need therefore to assure themselves of the reliability and quality of their suppliers. Increasingly organizations are only dealing with suppliers who meet very strict quality criteria. Indeed, companies who seek to comply with particular quality standards, such as the quality management standard BS5750, may find themselves forced to deal only with other organizations who meet the same standard. A similar principle applies with environmental protection. Companies which seek to benefit from a European eco-label, for example, will have to assure themselves that their suppliers are behaving in an environmentally responsible way. No organization can claim to be behaving in an environmentally sound fashion, if all its suppliers are sourced by companies which are excessive polluters. In this way purchasers will be pushing quality, consumer and environmental protection all the way down the supply chain.

As has been noted, one of the aims of the European exchange rate mechanism is to flatten out fluctuations in divergent exchange rates. Put very simply exchange rate volatility is swopped for interest rate volatility. As the economies of the Community converge there will be greater and longer periods of stability, culminating in irrevocable monetary union. This will remove one of the greatest risks facing managers purchasing across frontiers. The potential for a satisfactory deal negotiated for a good or service at a competitive rate to be ruined by a sharp adverse swing in the exchange rate has, in the past been not inconsiderable. Of course, hedging instruments are available for managers wishing to cover the potential downside which may result in an effective price increase between agreeing a contract, and paying for the goods or services, but these have tended to be expensive, are often complex, and are rarely accessible by smaller organizations. Whether or not purchases are being made from or to a member state which is a member of the exchange rate mechanism, or has advanced further down the road to economic and monetary union than others, one immediate tactic which purchasers can, and are increasingly applying is to negotiate supply contracts in ecus. As a basket of all the European currencies, it is intrinsically less liable to fluctuate significantly against one currency, than any other single currency, thus benefiting the supplier and purchaser by offering some degree of certainty as to the value of the final payments to be made.

A final point which needs to be considered is the issue of late payment of debt. Legislation and practice throughout the Community vary considerably, with most member states, unlike the UK, having some kind of statutory regime governing payment practice. These range from rights to interest on late payment, to greater enforceability of contract, and in some instances, a criminal liability for late payment. Suppliers should make themselves aware of prevalent and customary practice wherever they are purchasing, as well as their particular compliance requirements. The European Commission is currently considering whether or not there is scope for harmonizing late payment regulations, but the potential remains limited, and is certainly unlikely to be progressed for some time. However, managers, dependent on their suppliers for quality goods and services, will find it in their own interests to build up creditable relationships with those suppliers. Prompt payment will be a crucial part of that process.

23 Location

It has long been held a truism in retailing that there are three secrets of success: location, location and location. Previous chapters have explored the impact of the single market from a number of different perspectives – political, commercial, industrial and environmental. It is, however, useful to see the development of the internal market in terms of economic geography: location impinging on most areas of management decision. In this sense this section on location can be seen as summarizing the foregoing.

The free movement of people, goods and capital widens the locational choice. The siting of industry and businesses have, in the past, had less to do with commercial or economic sense, than cultural and historical perspectives. Individuals starting their own businesses will typically choose to commence operations in an area that they know well, or may have researched, before venturing further afield. For organizations that have been established some time, the horizon for new locations has often been limited to national boundaries because of the inherent problems of crossing frontiers. With these problems being, to a large extent, swept away, those horizons are pushed back, leaving wider choice, but other factors to be considered. Whatever type, age or size of operation is being considered, there are opportunities for increasing competitiveness and effectiveness, as well as economy in careful examination of the locational possibilities. The more obvious conclusions may not be the right ones, and there are also structural implications possibly through dispersal of activities. In very simple terms, the elements that go into a business operation, finance, raw materials, employees, processes and production, distribution, service and customers, as well as the peripheral activities like administration, public relations and research and development, are rarely in one place, and it is the task of the manager to link or bring them all together in a chain or network that is efficient and profitable. In some ways this task is made easier through the completion of the internal market, because all these elements are, to a greater or lesser extent, mobile and increasingly moving about the territory of the EC.

The phenomenon of economic clustering has already been touched on in some detail, but provides the starting point for the evolution of economic geography in the Community. An emerging golden triangle at the core of Europe must be the focus of attention in a number of areas. Not only are the densest markets likely to be in this region, but there will also be clusters of suppliers, skilled labour, and efficient transport networks. On the other hand, this is a region where overhead costs are likely to be at their highest. Land and property prices will be at a premium, as will skilled labour. Transport congestion is likely to be at its worst with resultingly heavy on-costs for distribution. An immediate question must be faced as to whether an organization seeks to produce a high-cost but high added-value product or service, in which case proximity to the golden triangle may be appropriate.

At a more local level, careful consideration needs to be given to proximity to the resources needed. This may be the academic or intellectual excellence available in science parks, or simply access to a railway spur or trunk road. An awareness of where the industrial centres of excellence are in Europe will be essential. Companies developing new products will wish to be integrated into developing technologies, benefiting from the osmosis of ideas in a particular locality through close partnerships, collaborative ventures and the like.

Similarly the development of different modes of communications networks vary enormously throughout Europe. An organization which is reliant on postal services is unlikely to prosper where there is not an efficient and cheap service. Already we see much direct mail in the Community originating from The Netherlands. Similarly, where an organization makes heavy usage of telephones, being based in a high cost country such as Spain may not be economic.

Alternatively access to a particular target market sector or supplier may be more appropriate, but will need careful consideration as patterns are continually changing. A print buyer in the 1980s would have been well positioned in Italy, but over the past decade UK printers have worked themselves back into a more competitive position.

Of particular relevance to most organizations will be labour costs, which are clearly an element which depends largely on the types of labour needed. Within a single country particular skill shortages vary significantly from region to region. The South West of England, for example has suffered from endemic recruitment difficulties for skilled and professional labour. Skill pools are just as likely to cluster as other forms of economic activity – often around administrative or academic centres. On the other hand, if the labour need is for relatively unskilled employees, then there is little point in paying the high-wage rates demanded in the clusters. Different skills already evince themselves in clusters: without wishing to be overly stereotypical, the United Kingdom has a surfeit of accountants, whilst there is little shortage of engineers in Germany. There is an above average number of computer programmers in Ireland, but Germany suffers from a shortage of experienced construction workers. Italian studies have shown a shortage of skilled workers in the clothing sector, shortages of nurses are commonplace throughout the Community, and so on. An essential point to understand is that once an appreciation of geography is grasped, the options continue to open up: whether to move the work to the resource, the resource to the work, or simply to keep them apart and make best available use of the developing trans-European networks. The decision will vary from organization to organization, and resource to resource.

Energy, for example, is in some of its forms, one of the most highly mobile resources that there are. Electricity can move across large distances at little cost. Gas, on the other hand is much more expensive, and even within the UK companies in Wales pay more for their gas than companies on the East Coast who are nearer to the North Sea gas fields. Energy intensive companies will need to consider carefully where their sources should be, but again the answer may not be simply to locate near the closest available source of energy. UK steel manufacturers are already finding that it is cheaper to import coal than to buy it from neighbouring coal fields. Similarly there are wide divergences in electricity prices across the Community. Maximizing the comparative advantage with the appropriate mix of benefits is all in the locational decision.

A further factor which should not be ignored is the intervention of government and its agencies. National governments, the European Commission, regional development authorities and so on, are all actively seeking to distort locational decision-making to encourage companies to locate in depressed areas. Grants, subsidies and other incentives are all available, but should be treated with caution. If a company needs an artificial incentive to locate somewhere other than where commercial logic suggests, the incentive needs to be carefully weighed up against the disadvantages.

The factors impinging on the specific aspects of distribution, marketing and service do not need to be repeated. Access to appropriate transport networks will clearly be essential. Similarly there are significant considerations as to whether a physical presence is necessary in the market to promote a particular product or service, and indeed to service that product. In many cases the decision as to location will involve a dispersal of activities. Typically a head office function will need to be near to an administrative centre; a production site near to an efficient transport network, supplier or customer. If customers are wishing to involve suppliers in just-in-time techniques then proximity will be an essential, but the development of the transport network makes economically feasible all sorts of arrangements to mix better the comparative advantages. A German crisp maker has, for example, found it most efficient to buy potatoes in Belgium, transport them by lorry to Italy to be peeled, and then back to Germany to be fried. This may be an extreme possibility but exemplifies well the opportunities that should be taken. Back office operations rarely need to be near to suppliers or markets, and can be located at the most advantageous sites for keeping down property or labour costs, making the most of telecommunications networks. Research and development operations will benefit from being close to academic centres of excellence. Distribution sites will certainly need to be in immediate proximity to a link into the main arteries of the transport network, but not necessarily close to the market-place – Northern Ireland has proved to be an effective European distribution centre for a number of international organizations. The dispersed organization can best take advantage of the appropriate mix tapping into the relevant targeted clusters of resource. It is essential that every organization audits its activities to take stock of the opportunities being offered by the ability to range freely throughout the European territory. The rights of establishment and the rights to mobility for individuals, goods and services produce an entirely different recipe for business success. Not only are the ingredients different, but the means of putting them together have changed. Above all it is worth remembering that they will continue to change.

Notes

1   Bannock G. (1987) *Dictionary of Economics*, London: Hutchinson.
2   An international agreement now covering more than 100 countries, with a secretariat based in Geneva. Founded in 1947 with a view to reducing the numbers of tariffs and freeing trade through a system of reciprocal multilateralism whereby privileges and freedoms extended to one country (a most favoured nation (MFN)) should be extended to others. There have been six 'Rounds', with the Uruguay Round seeking to extend the GATT principles to a number of new areas including services.
3   Deloitte, Touche Tohmatsu International (September 1992) *Why companies go international?*
4   Goldin I. and van der Mensbrugghe D. (1992) *Trade Liberalisation: What's at stake*, Policy Brief No. 5, Paris, OECD Development Centre.
5   Ibid.
6   Unofficial translation. As the UK was not an original signatory to the Treaty of Rome there is no official translation of the treaty.
7   *The Regions in the 1990s*. Fourth Periodic Report of the European Commission. COM(90)609.
8   British Chambers of Commerce Discussion Paper (1990) *European Economic Integration and the Regions*.
9   European Free Trade Association. Initially United Kingdom, Portugal, Denmark, Norway, Sweden, Austria and Finland and Iceland. Following accession to the EC by first three, restricted to the remaining five, who now with the EC form the European Economic Area.
10   Association of South East Asian Nations. Indonesia, Malaysia, Philippines, Singapore and Thailand.
11   North American Free Trade Association – Canada, US, and Mexico.
12   Lomé Convention.
13   Heseltine M. (1989) *The Challenge of Europe*, London: Pan.
14   Article G(A)(i) of the Treaty on European Union replaced the term 'European Economic Community' by the term 'European Community' throughout the treaty. It is also common usage. More accurately the term 'European Communities' should be used, as the institutions of the Community are responsible for the Economic Community, Euratom, and European Coal and Steel Community.
15   Ibid.
16   The 'democratic deficit' which came into common usage following the European Parliament's report into European Union, which was the precursor to the Maastricht Treaty, and refers to the (then) lack of powers available to the democratically elected representatives in the European Parliament, underlining that power in the Community rests largely with unelected commissioners, and the unaccountable Council of Ministers who do not have to refer decisions to their own national parliaments.

17 COM(85)310, Brussels, 14 June 1985.
18 Marleasing SA v. La Comercial Internacional de Alimentación SA.
19 Treaty on European Union, Preamble.
20 Ibid, Art. 123.
21 Ibid, Art. 126.
22 Ibid, Art. 129a.
23 Ibid, Art. 130.
24 Ibid, Art. 130f.
25 The European Economic Area introduces Single Market legislation into countries outside the EC to stimulate free trade, but does not bind EEA members to the whole of the *acquis communautaire*, the entire code of EC legislation.
26 Paola Cecchini, *The European Challenge — Benefits of a single market*. For further information on the benefits of a single market, see 'The Costs of Non-Europe' a detailed sectoral examination published by the European Commission. It should be noted that more up-to-date calculations now exist, and that the Cecchini figures were only approximations designed to motivate completion of the single market.
27 The Ruding Report on Corporation Tax for example.
28 91/680/EEC.
29 Commission of the European Communities. *Guide to VAT in 1993*.
30 Coulson-Thomas C. and Brown R. (1990) *The Responsive Organisation*, London: BIM.
31 Hornby D. (1990) *The European Marketplace*. London: Macmillan.
32 European Council Declaration (5 December 1978) Brussels.
33 Treaty on European Union, Article 104c.
34 Porter M. (1990) *Competitive Advantage of Nations*, London: Macmillan.
35 Ibid, p. xii.
36 4064/89, OJ L 395 1989.
37 If a treaty requirement is worded unconditionally, is self-sufficient and legally complete so that its implementation or validity requires no further intervention by member states it can apply directly to individuals. [Ruling of the European Court of Justice, Case 26/62 Van Gend & Loos, 1963, ECR1.]
38 The sale of goods on a foreign market at a price below the marginal cost, often carried out to achieve market penetration, or to threaten existing competitors.
39 In this instance, companies with fewer than 150 employees or an annual turnover of less than 150 million ecus.
40 Source: *Daily Telegraph*, 25/9/92.
41 *Industrial policy in an open and competitive environment*, European Commission Communication to the Council and European Parliament.
42 Some economists suggest that the more likely distribution will be a golden banana stretching from the north of Germany, through the Benelux to the Ile de France, and down into northern Italy.
43 Treaty on European Union, Art. 130a.
44 Coulson-Thomas C. and S. (1990) *Implementing a Telecommuting Programme*, London: Rank Xerox.
45 British Chambers of Commerce (1992) *European Economic Integration and the Regions*, Discussion Paper, London: BCC.
46 European Commission, *Europe 2000 — Outlook for the Development of the Community's Territory*, COM(90)544.

47 Ibid.
48 European Agricultural Guidance and Guarantee Fund (EAGGF – the principal instrument of the Common Agricultural Policy); European Social Fund (ESF); and European Regional Development Fund (ERDF).
49 Treaty on European Union, Protocol on Economic and Social Cohesion.
50 Social Europe 3/90, European Commission, 1991.
51 Commission Opinion of 21 October 1990 COM(90)600 and SEC (91) 500.
52 Treaty on European Union, Article 118a(2).
53 Ibid, Article 123.
54 Agreement on social policy concluded between the member states of the European Community with the exception of the United Kingdom of Great Britain and Northern Ireland, annexed to the Treaty on European Union.
55 Article 100A of the Single European Act which is the legal basis for harmonization of legislation required for completion of the internal market requires this to be set at the highest level.
56 EEC/85/374.
57 EEC/84/450.
58 This threshold is subject to downwards revision as it is governed by the GATT Government Procurement Agreement.
59 *Selling to Europe* (1990) NEDO.
60 European Commission, *Europe 2000*, COM(91)452.
61 Treaty on European Union, Article 129b.
62 *The Global Telecommunications traffic boom*. IIC Research Report, G. C. Staple, 1990.
63 Treaty on European Union, Articles 2 & 3(k).
64 Suggested further reading includes:
    – Peppercorn G. and Skoulding G. (1987) *A Profile of British Industry*, BIM.
    – Coulson-Thomas C. (1989) *The New Professionals*, BIM/Aston University.
    – *The Effective Head Office*, (1988) BIM/Cresap.
65 Coulson-Thomas C. and Brown R. (1989) *The Responsive Organisation*, British Institute of Management.
66 EEC/68/151.
67 EEC/77/91.
68 EEC/78/855.
69 EEC/78/660.
70 The European Commission has more than a hundred different definitions of a small and medium sized enterprises appropriate to different programmes, and regulations. In this instance, a small enterprise is defined as one that does not exceed two of the following three criteria (the thresholds for medium-sized companies are in brackets):
    1 a balance sheet of 1,550,000 (6,200,000) ecus
    2 a net turnover of 3,200,00 (12,800,000) ecus
    3 an average of 50 (250) employees during the year in question.
71 COM(90)629.
72 Brown R. and Rycroft T. (1988) *Involved in Europe*. London: BIM.
73 EEC/82/891.
74 EEC/83/849.
75 EEC/84/253.

76 EEC/89/666.
77 EEC/89/667.
78 Toffler A. (1971) *Future Shock*. London: Pan.
79 EEC/79/129.
80 EEC/77/187.
81 EEC/80/987.
82 EEC/75/117.
83 EEC/76/207.
84 EEC/86/378.
85 EEC/86/613.
86 There remains considerable uncertainty as to the eventual impact of this judgement. Controversy surrounds the ability, and cost, of the court's decision to impose equal pension benefits retroactively. A protocol to the Maastricht Treaty attempts to confine the impact of the judgement to benefits earned from the day of the judgement (17 May 1991), but not before.
87 Social Europe, 3/90, European Commission.
88 Coulson-Thomas C. and Brown R. (1989) *The Responsive Organisation*, BIM.
89 COM(92)2000.
90 Pilotti L. and Pozzana R. (1991) *Franchising Contracts in the European Community*, European Commission Study No 18.
91 AEG, Bull, GCE, GEC, ICL, Nixdorf, Olivetti, Philips, Plessey, Siemens, Thomson.
92 Lord Young, Chairman Cable & Wireless, LBC interview 26.9.92.
93 The *Daily Telegraph*, September 25, 1992, p. 17.
94 Helme M., ed. (1991) *Managing IT for competitive advantage*. BIM.
95 Coulson-Thomas C. and S. (1991) *Implementing a telecommuting programme*. Adaptation Ltd.
96 L382 21/12/86 & 18/7/89.
97 *Single Market News* (Autumn 1992). Issue No 16.
98 EEC/88/361.
99 COM(88)778.

Selected bibliography

Brown R. (1991). *Doing Business in Europe*. London: Hodder & Stoughton.
Roney A. (1992). *The European Community Fact Book*. London: Kogan Page.
Brown R. (1992). *Managing in Europe*. BIM.
Brewster & Teague (1989). *EC Social Policy*. IPM.
Brown M. (1990). *Economic and Monetary Union*. BIM.
Brown R. (1989). *The European Employer*. BIM.
Brown R. (1990). *Involved in Europe*. BIM.
Andrew J. (1992). *Employment Law in the European Community*. London: Kogan Page.
Budd S. (1989). *A Guide to the Maze*. London: Kogan Page.
Cecchini P. (1988). *The European Challenge*. Wildwood House.
CBI (1990). *Employment and Training*. Mercury.
CRONER (1991). *Croners' Europe*.
Coulson-Thomas C. & Brown R. (1990). *The Responsive Organisation*. BIM.
EUROMONITOR, 1992. (1989). *The Single Market Handbook*.
Rajan A. (1990). *1992: A Zero Sum Game*. Industrial Society.

Index